Stitches, Patterns and Projects for Needlecraft

Also by Wanda Bonando
Stitches, Patterns and Projects for Knitting
Stitches, Patterns and Projects for Crocheting

STITCHES, PATTERNS AND PROJECTS FOR
NEEDLECRAFT

Originally published in Italian in 1981 by Arnoldo
Mondadori Editore S.p.A., Milan under the title *Guida al
Ricamo*

Copyright © 1981 Arnoldo Mondadori Editore S.p.A., Milan
English translation copyright © 1984 Arnoldo Mondadori
Editore S.p.A., Milan

Translated by Sylvia Mulcahy

FIRST U.S. EDITION

Library of Congress Cataloging in Publication Data

Bonando, Wanda.
    Stitches, patterns and projects for needlecraft.
    (Harper colophon books; CN 1096)
    Translation of: Guida al ricamo.
    1. Needlework. I. Nava, Marinella. II. Title.
TT750.B6613 1984   746.44   83-48329
ISBN 0-06-091096-8 (pbk.)

84 85 86 10 9 8 7 6 5 4 3 2 1

Printed in Italy by Arnoldo Mondadori Editore, Verona

WANDA BONANDO
MARINELLA NAVA

Stitches, Patterns and Projects for Needlecraft

HARPER COLOPHON BOOKS

HARPER & ROW, PUBLISHERS

NEW YORK, CAMBRIDGE, PHILADELPHIA, SAN FRANCISCO

LONDON, MEXICO CITY, SAO PAULO, SYDNEY

Contents

The authors wish to thank Anna Clima and Augusta Fabbri
for their kind collaboration.
The sculpture shown on page 223 is by Renzo Apruzzese.

To write the history of embroidery would involve a long journey back through time. It is a history that is not only closely linked to custom and fashion but also to art through the ages as well as to near and far civilizations, from Ancient Greece to the Far East and from the Americas to Europe.

This ancient decorative technique, with its humble origins, has undergone phases of increasing elaboration, with embellishments of all kinds, as the centuries have passed and civilizations have come and gone. Its application, too, has known many changes. It has played its part in highlighting the magnificence of courts and palaces, in adding to the significance of sacred vestments and hangings, in emphasizing the dignity of uniforms and, not least, in beautifying the trousseaux of untold numbers of brides.

The golden age of embroidery is now over, but the art has never ceased to be practiced, in its rather more minor forms, in the pursuit of those exquisitely feminine touches that still mean so much in any home. The craft is experiencing a revival at the moment and it is hoped that this manual will make a small contribution to this trend.

The authors' aims are twofold. One is to provide the less expert embroiderer with all the basic knowledge needed to improve her (or his) skills. The other is to give a new impetus to the more experienced needlewoman, with ideas and explanations for making things which, up to now, she may have regarded as a little too difficult but which are in fact very worthwhile.

The text, which is liberally illustrated with diagrams and photographs, is divided into four sections. In the first, techniques and basic stitches are shown; in the second, a wide range of stitches, from the simplest to the most elaborate, are explained, making it possible for almost any decorative motif to be worked. Particular care has been taken to ensure that the instructions for each stitch are close to the relevant diagram so that the method of working is quite clear.

The third section covers things to make, including some traditional and some new ideas. Here, too, each description is illustrated by a color photograph of the finished article and there is a detailed diagram for every motif.

In the fourth and last section are several series of the letters of the alphabet and of sample monograms. The charming habit of trimming sheets, pillowcases, towels, nightgowns and lingerie with the initials of the owner may be old-fashioned but it has certainly made a comeback, with a few new ideas for application as well, in this age of mass-production. Most people are seeking to have something that is distinctive.

From the needle to embroidery frame: materials, equipment and techniques

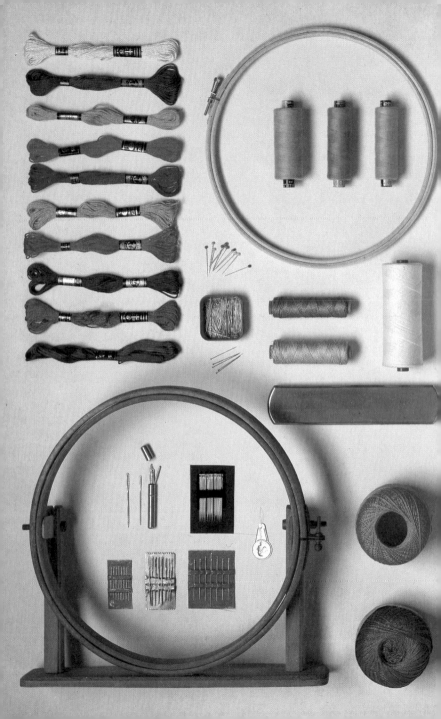

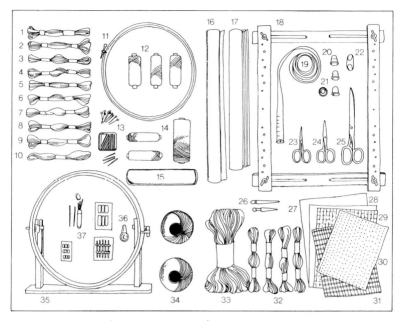

On the two preceding pages you will see illustrated all the equipment needed to do every type of embroidery. Each item is referred to, sometimes several times, in the text. In the above diagram, which has been made from the photograph, each item has been numbered to correspond with the list that follows, to enable you to identify it.

1–10 skeins of stranded cotton
11 embroidery hoop or ring
12 thick sewing thread
13 various types of pins
14 thick shaded sewing thread
15 heavy brass weight
16 tracing paper
17 waxed paper
18 square frame
19 tape measure
20 dressmakers' thimbles (closed)
21 tailors' thimbles (open)
22 fingerguard
23 small curved scissors
24 embroidery scissors
25 cutting-out shears
26 embroidery stilettos
27 embroidery linen
28 fine embroidery linen
29 double thread canvas – coarse weave
30 double thread canvas – fine weave
31 single thread canvas – fine weave
32 skein of soft embroidery cotton
33 skein of cotton for canvas work
34 balls of "perlé" cotton
35 circular embroidery frame with tablestand
36 needle-threader
37 various sized steel needles

THE NEEDLE

The needle-threader
This is a small but very useful piece of equipment. Having inserted the metal loop into the eye of the needle, pass the thread through the loop and withdraw the threader.

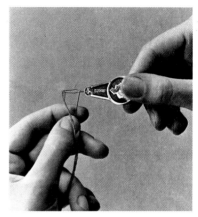

To work on right side of material
In order to work on the right side of the material, first make a small stitch on the wrong side. Now draw the needle through from the wrong to the right side at the point from which the embroidery is to start.

To bring needle through from right to left
With the thread on the right side of the work, pass the needle through to the wrong side with the needle pointing from right to left. Take up a small piece of the fabric and draw thread through from the right side.

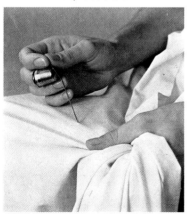

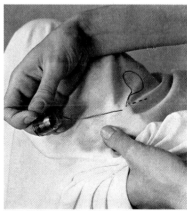

To bring needle through from left to right

Follow the previous instruction but with the needle pointing from left to right.

To bring needle through downwards

Follow the previous instruction but with the needle entering the fabric vertically downwards.

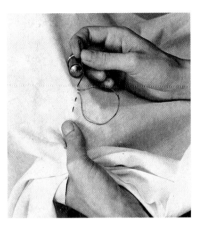
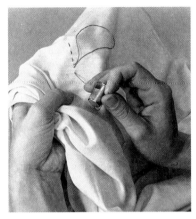
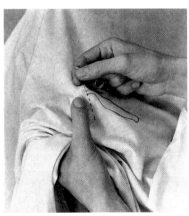
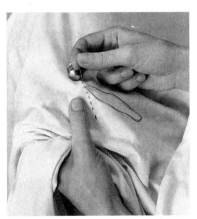

To bring needle through upwards

Follow the previous instruction but with the needle pointing vertically upwards.

To bring needle through slanting towards the right

Follow the previous instruction but slant the needle towards the right.

To bring needle through slanting towards the left
Follow the previous instruction but slant the needle towards the left.

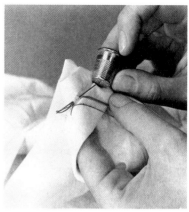

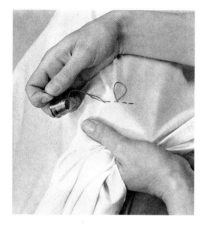

To bring needle through eye foremost
Sometimes, when working on very fine fabric – as in drawn threadwork – the needle point can break the threads. In this case, use the needle so that the eye enters the fabric first.

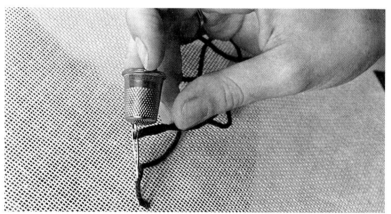

Wool and canvas needles
Generally known as tapestry needles, they have a rounded end and a rather broad eye to facilitate insertion.

Proportion between needle and thread

Needle and thread must always be in proportion otherwise the thread may break or slip out of the eye. They must also be in proportion with the fabric; if too thick, they will make unsightly holes (illustration below right); if too fine, the embroidery will not stand out. Below, left: correct proportions are illustrated.

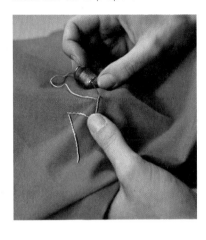

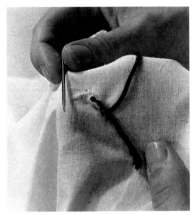

THE THREAD

On right side of work

It is the left thumb that always holds the work firm on the right side, whether it has to be to the left of the needle or to the right.

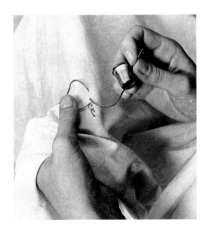

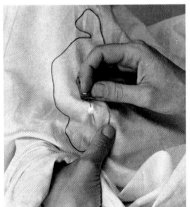

Over the needle

The expression "thread over needle" refers to the thread being at the eye end of the needle, in a vertical stitch, or over the point of the needle in a horizontal stitch.

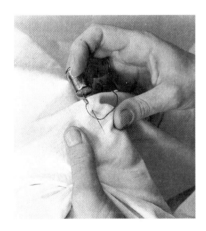
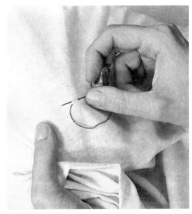

Under the needle

The expression "under needle" or "under point of needle" refers to the thread when it forms a loop under the point of the needle, in a vertical stitch, or when it is below the needle, in a horizontal stitch.

Thread round needle

The thread is taken one or more times round the needle, on the right side of work, to form a decorative knot.

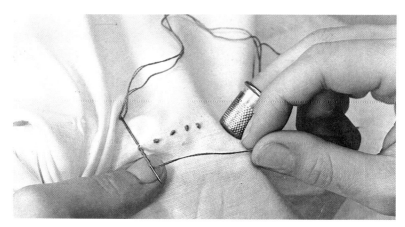

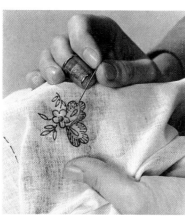

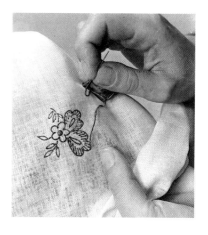

Passing from one stitch to another

For short distances, thread can be carried over on the back, otherwise finish off securely and start again, on the back, for the new stitch.

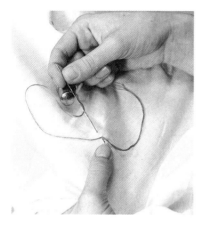
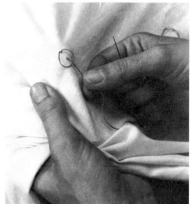

Drawing thread upwards (or downwards)

The expression "draw thread upwards (or downwards)" refers to the
need to carry out this action in relation to the stitch itself.

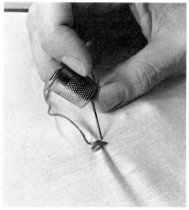

Correct tension of thread

When the thread is drawn through
correctly, the stitch remains well
seated without pulling the fabric in
any way, a fault which cannot be
rectified even with ironing. The
photographs illustrate, above left,
the correct tension of thread and,
above right, faulty tension.

Fastening off

When you reach the end of a length of thread or need to break off and restart, take the needle through to the back of the work and make a few tiny, invisible stitches.

Cutting the thread

When the fastening off has been carefully completed on the back of work, cut the thread with very sharp embroidery scissors.

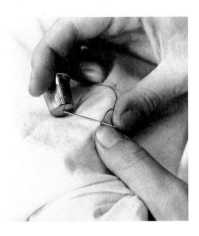

SCISSORS

Long, straight blades

When cutting fabric, use very sharp scissors with long, straight blades. An ideal length for cutting-out shears is $8\frac{1}{4}$ in (21 cm). It is important not to pull or fray the material.

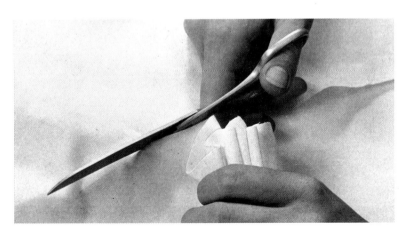

Small with straight pointed blades

Small scissors with straight, pointed blades are called embroidery scissors and are only used to cut the thread, both from the skein or ball and in the needle.

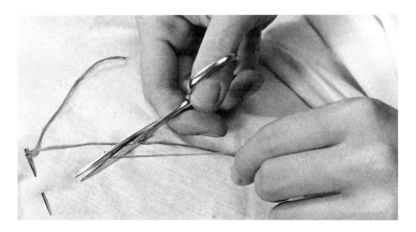

Small with curved blades

Small scissors with curved blades are used to remove surplus fabric when scalloped or fancy edges are required and basic buttonhole stitch is being used (see page 42), for a corded edge (see page 42) and for open-work embroidery as in broderie anglaise (see page 72) or guipure (cut out) work (see page 86). Unsuitable scissors could ruin work, see photograph (above right).

OTHER EQUIPMENT

Pins

Pins are used every time one piece of fabric has to be held firmly on to another or when waxed paper is being used as a backing, etc. They are also useful as markers and to indicate the right and wrong side of a fabric. It is important for them to be fine, rust-proof and to have sharp points.

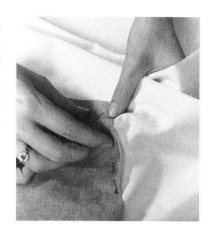

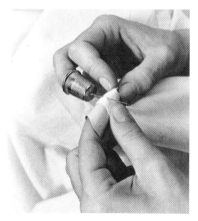

Tape measure

The tape measure is usually 60 in (150 cm) long. It is important for it to have clear numbers and markings, and it should be made of a tough, non-stretch material.

Fingerguard

The fingerguard is worn on the finger of the left hand that supports the work from the back. It saves the finger from being pricked.

Thimble

The thimble is a metal or plastic cap that fits over the top of the middle finger of the right hand. It is used to push the needle through the fabric and thus avoid damage to the finger.

The open, or tailors', thimble serves the same purpose. It is important for a thimble to be the right size – neither too tight, nor too loose.

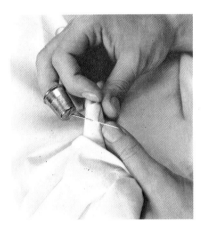 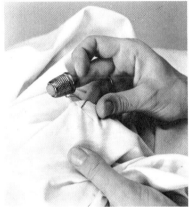

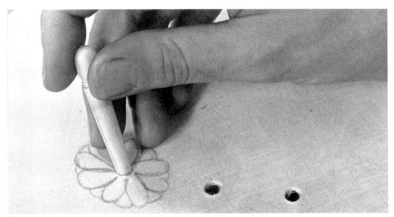

Punch

The punch is a pointed tool made of metal, bone or wood. It is used to make small holes, as for example in broderie anglaise (see page 72), which are finished off in basic buttonhole stitch (see page 42) or straight overcasting (see page 41).

Waxed paper

Waxed paper is used as a backing to give body to the fabric to be embroidered. In the case of Renaissance work (see page 88), it acts as a firm base on which to work the bars. Waxed paper is easy to remove and can even be used again.

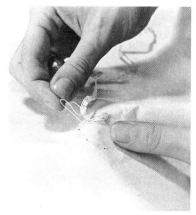

EMBROIDERY FRAMES

Embroidery frames are used to hold the fabric taut while it is being embroidered and to ensure the stitches are even. There are two types, circular and square, the choice depending upon the type of work and its size.

How to use the circular embroidery frame or hoop

The circular frame consists of two rings of wood or plastic which fit into each other. The larger ring has an opening which enables it to be tightened or loosened by means of a screw.

To keep the fabric in place in the frame, place over the smaller ring and surround with the larger one (2); tighten the screw until the fabric is taut. There is no need to pull the fabric once tightly secured in the

4

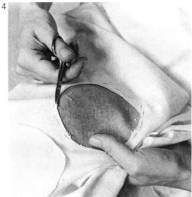

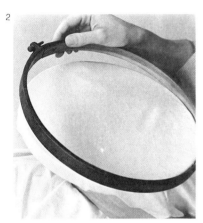

A stand can usually be fitted to the frame so that the work can stand on a table or on the embroiderer's knee. The right hand then stays in front of the work while the left stays behind to guide the needle from the back to the front (5).

frame as it could become distorted.

If the fabric is too small to fit the ring, it should be basted onto a larger piece of fabric and the backing material cut away (4). The work can now be mounted (3).

Mounting your fabric on a frame

A stretcher frame consists of two sets of two connecting wooden strips which when joined at the corners form the frame. They are

available in craft and art supply stores in a variety of sizes. Select a frame whose inside opening measures slightly larger than the finished area of your fabric. Center the fabric, stamped side down, against the back of the frame. Using thumbtacks or staples begin by anchoring the corners of the fabric to the frame. Then, pulling the fabric taut, securely attach each side of the fabric to the frame. An advantage to using a stretcher frame is that your work is framed as you complete it and ready to hang the minute it is finished. If the fabric slackens as you work simply remove a tack or two, pull the fabric tight and reattach.

A scroll frame is not available in as many sizes as a stretcher frame, but it will keep the fabric taut at all times. Scroll frames can only accommodate the same or smaller width fabric than the width of the frame. Available in widths of 18 in (45.7 cm) 24 in (61 cm) and 36 in (91.4 cm), scroll frames usually have side arms 18 in (45.7 cm) long. To attach the fabric to the scroll frame stitch it to both top and side rods (see illustration opposite). Then firmly attach the rods to the side arms, weaving one side tightly to the frame as shown below.

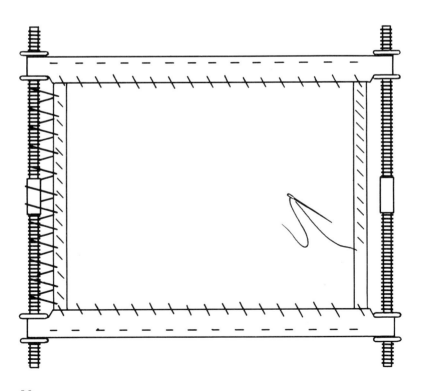

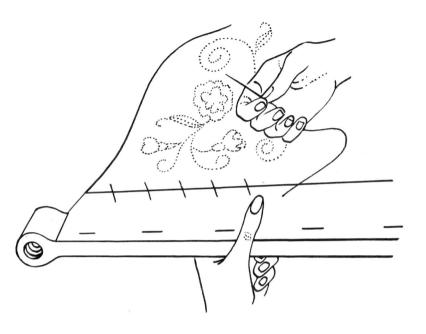

FABRICS

Choosing the correct stitch and embroidery thread for the material

Every type of fabric, whether it be cotton or canvas, satin or fine linen, wool or velvet, can be embroidered providing it has sufficient elasticity to allow a needle and thread to pass through it. At the same time, it must be strong enough not only to hold the stitches but also not to be damaged while it is being worked. It is therefore possible to visualize, on any fabric, some way in which a design or decorative motif could be reproduced. Sometimes a fabric which already has a printed or machine-embroidered pattern on it may inspire further ideas, using the existing design as a guide, either as outlines or as a background, for a new piece of embroidery.

While it can be said that in general embroidery can be worked on all types of fabric, it should be remembered that, although the fabric always acts as a base, it has its own distinctive features. First of all there is the nature of the weave itself; then there is the thickness, strength, weight, color, texture, etc. Before you decide on which combination of characteristics you require, therefore, it is important to consider what stitch(es) you are going to use and what type of embroidery thread.

The choice of stitch and of thread must always depend on the fabric. They are entirely complementary to each other and it would obviously be as inadvisable to use a thick embroidery thread on a delicate, lightweight fabric as it would be to use a very fine thread on a heavy fabric or an open weave. It is equally inappropriate to use a very closely worked stitch – especially over a wide area – on a fine fabric; even if the thread were of suitable thickness, the fabric would be unable to support the embroidery.

One or two warnings will be useful at this stage. Generally speaking, fabrics should not be washed before any embroidery is worked on them. This advice is particularly relevant to new fabrics which invariably contain a good deal of dressing to give them body. And, finally, fabrics should always be cut with scissors rather than ripped; this applies particularly to all types of canvas, linen (whether coarse or fine), sailcloth and burlap.

Choosing the correct stitch and embroidery thread for the canvas

Canvas, in its various forms, is the fabric that is used as a base for needlepoint, also known as canvaswork or tapestry, to be made up into such things as wall-hangings, floor rugs, chair and cushion covers, etc., and can be bought by the yard (or by the meter, in some countries) in a variety of widths. It provides a durable foundation and usually contains quite a lot of dressing to hold the mesh in position; the mesh is obtainable in different sizes, according to the thickness of the canvas. Three types are normally available from the suppliers: plain and interlock mono or single thread canvas, double thread or Penelope canvas (the mesh being formed by the warp and weft being arranged in pairs) and rug canvas which is large gauge and used mainly for gros-point, Smyrna stitch or latch-hooking. As the canvas is quite stiff to work on and the square mesh is easy to see, even complicated designs are easy to reproduce. To facilitate the work

even further, canvases with designs already printed on them in recommended colors can also be bought.

The type of canvas to choose obviously depends on the type of work you are planning to undertake and especially the stitch or stitches you would like to use, bearing in mind that a number of stitches are difficult, if not impossible, to execute on certain types of canvas. Another important point to remember is that the size of mesh and thickness of the canvas should be in proportion to the weight of yarn to be used. If the yarn is too fine in relation to the size of mesh and thickness of the canvas the stitches will not cover it. If the yarn is too thick, the stitches will be too tight and the canvas will pucker.

Needlepoint should always be worked on a square frame to ensure that the stitches are as even as pos-

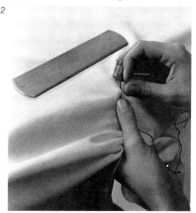

sible. Canvas should never be dampened, not even when the work is completed. To remove any marks it is best to go to a dry-cleaner but cleaning should be undertaken as infrequently as possible. Regular gentle brushing with a soft brush should keep the finished article fresh.

How to get the best results with your embroidery

The success of embroidery depends largely on two factors: the way in which the fabric is held and the evenness of the tension. It is relatively easy to maintain the right tension between fabric and stitches when an embroidery frame is used. If the piece of fabric to be embroidered is rather small and no frame is being used, the part to be embroidered should be placed over the index finger – protected by a fingerguard – of the left hand (1). If the piece of fabric is large, it is a good idea to place a weight (2) on the part not being embroidered.

When embroidering light-colored fabrics or very large pieces, protect all the fabric not actually being worked on by covering it with tissue paper or some other light material.

How to get the best results with your needlepoint

Needlepoint, being worked on canvas, should always be mounted on a stretcher or scroll frame assembled as described on pages 25–27. By working in this way, providing the frame is the right size to take the whole piece of canvas, there will be no danger of it becoming distorted as work progresses. It is possible to do canvaswork without a frame, but if the canvas is large the piece of canvas not being worked should be weighted down on a table.

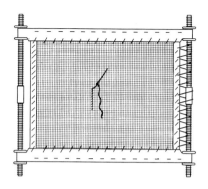

WASHING AND IRONING EMBROIDERY

Washing white embroidery

Washing embroidery is one of the most important and delicate operations.

White cotton fabric, embroidered in white, should be washed by hand in hot water with a good liquid detergent. If very dirty, squeeze firmly but avoid rubbing as this might damage the threads of the embroidery. Rinse gently in cold, running water. If there are any stubborn marks, this type of embroidery may be left in a solution of bleach (for quantities, see instructions on bottle) for about 30 minutes. Rinse thoroughly in cold, running water.

Any white cotton articles, embroidered in white, should be allowed to dry in the open air.

Washing colored embroidery

The first thing to be done when washing colored embroidery is to soak a piece of cotton in hot water and press it on to the various colored parts of the article to make sure that no color comes out of either the fabric or the embroidery. Even if only one of the colors shows signs of running, dry-cleaning will be the only answer.

If the colors prove to be fast washing can proceed as follows. Dissolve some mild white soap flakes in hot water and work up a good lather; now add cold water to bring the temperature down to about 86°F (30°C). Immerse the embroidered article and move it about gently in the soapy water without, on any account, rubbing it. Rinse well in lukewarm water and then in cold, running water until the water runs clear.

Remove the article from the water and, without wringing or squeezing, place on a clean, dry towel. Turn one end of the towel over the top of the article and roll up carefully, with the towel on the outside. Pat gently so that all surplus water is absorbed by the towel, unroll and hang the embroidered article up to dry.

Particularly delicate embroidery may be left to soak in warm, salt water for 8 hours before washing as described above.

Embroidery on woolen fabrics requires special care. Such articles should be washed in cold water with a special liquid detergent for wool and dried flat between two cloths away from direct heat and, if out of doors, in the shade.

Ironing

Another important operation is ironing embroidery. It must always be ironed on the wrong side over a well-padded surface to ensure that the right side of the embroidery does not become flattened (1). The temperature of the iron should be appropriate to the fabric being ironed – very hot for linens and cottons, warm for silk, wool and velvets. The fabric should never be completely dry and a damp cloth (2) or fine spray may be used. A steam iron is particularly useful when ironing embroidery but, when dealing with canvas or fabrics such as silk, velvet and wool, it should be held slightly raised off the article.

1

2

REPRODUCTION TECHNIQUES FOR DESIGNS AND MOTIFS

We have already mentioned that canvases and other types of fabric can be obtained with the design (and indications as to color) already printed on them, though anyone with an inventive mind can make his or her own designs or motifs. Before describing the several methods of reproduction onto fabrics, it should be understood that there are two categories of design:

a) those with curved lines, drawn free-hand, and
b) counted-thread designs and decorative graphic and geometric motifs.

One of the most common reproduction techniques is to trace a design already drawn on paper, preferably tissue paper, by using carbon paper. The risk of smudging or marking the fabric with the carbon paper can be overcome by using special dressmakers' carbon which is yellow for light-colored fabrics and white for dark fabrics. This technique gives excellent results on smooth fabrics.

Another method is to obtain pre-printed transfers which can then be ironed onto the fabric with a fairly hot iron; it must be remembered, however, that these designs, which are prepared on very thin paper with a special ink, will then be reproduced in reverse, like a mirror image.

A system which gives excellent results on any fabric involves the use of powdered charcoal or pounce, which may be white or colored, and a tracing wheel. As the wheel is guided over the design, which should be on tracing paper, it perforates the outlines and the powder or pounce reproduces the design on the fabric. The outline can then be fixed by going over it with a fine paintbrush and opaque paint, a dressmaker's pencil or a soft-tipped felt pen. The advantage of this method is that the tracing paper can be used several times.

When fine, light-colored fabrics are being used, designs can be traced directly onto the fabric which is merely placed over the design. With thick or dark fabric the design can be placed on glass – such as a windowpane, glass-topped table (with a source of light coming from beneath), etc., so that, as the light shines through, the design can be traced.

Also available are designs printed on thin paper in special inks which can be rubbed onto the fabric with the thumbnail. This type of transfer can only be used once.

Geometric motifs and designs worked on counted threads are simpler. They are nearly always already worked out on a grid and are thus easy to follow or to adapt to one's own requirements.

Tracing with carbon paper

The design is placed over the fabric with a piece of dressmaker's carbon paper inserted in between. Hold in position with pins or drawing pins. Trace all the outlines of the design with a fairly soft pencil, taking care not to tear or make holes in the paper. Before lifting the tracing paper off, it is important to make sure that all the lines have been reproduced accurately.

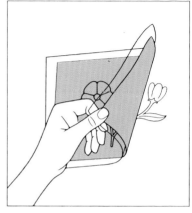

Ironing on a transfer

Place the transfer on the fabric with the rougher side downwards. It is important not to move the iron while the design is being transferred. The temperature of the iron should be appropriate to the type of fabric on which the design is being reproduced in order to achieve a perfect result without running the risk of scorching the fabric.

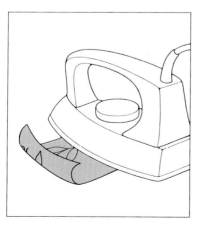

Tracing with powder

With a needle or tracing wheel (not illustrated), follow around all outlines of the design to give regular, small perforations. Take care not to overlook any of the details (1). Now place the perforated paper over the fabric and, by using a firm powderpuff or blackboard eraser, spread charcoal powder or pounce, a powder specially made for this purpose, all over the paper, making sure it

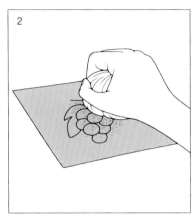

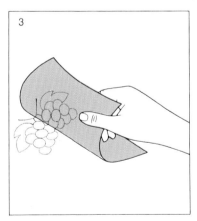

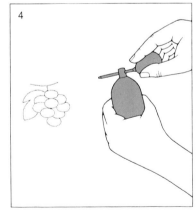

penetrates all the holes (2). Lift the tracing paper carefully, checking that the design has been reproduced completely (3). Go over the design with a brush and opaque paint, a dressmaker's pencil or a soft-tipped felt marker, or fix with alcohol fixative (4).

Alcohol fixative is not available in the United States.

Tracing over glass

Put the piece of paper, with the design you wish to reproduce, on a piece of glass where there is some source of light from underneath such as a window or a glass-topped illuminated table, keeping it in position as illustrated. Place the fabric over design, which will show through quite clearly, hold it firmly in place and go over the outline with a soft pencil.

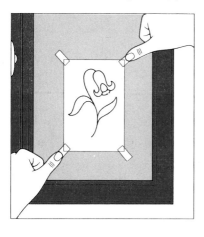

Thumbnail transference

Using a printed transfer, place it with the inked side downwards onto the fabric on a firm, flat surface. With the thumbnail rub firmly along every line in order to transfer the inked design onto the fabric. Before removing the transfer sheet completely, lift it up carefully to make sure that the design has been perfectly reproduced. If there are any weak parts, simply repeat the operation.

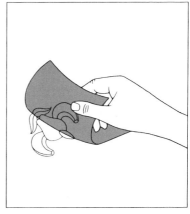

How to reduce or enlarge a design

The first step in reducing or enlarging a design or geometric motif is to mark out the design itself into squares. Secondly, by redrawing the design or motif over the same number of smaller or larger squares, it can easily be adjusted to the right size.

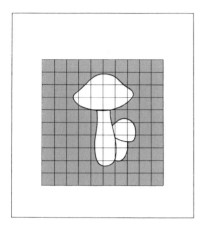

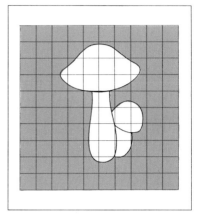

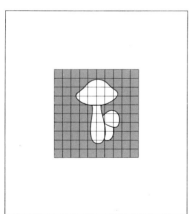

Symmetrical reproduction on a corner

In order to make a motif or design fit symmetrically into a corner, place a mirror on the printed transfer or drawing, adjusting its position until

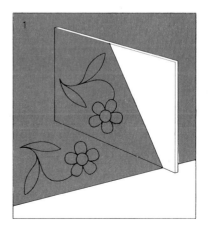

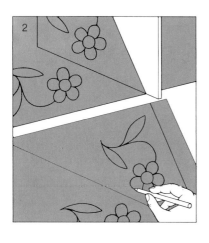

it reflects the required corner arrangement (1). Mark the angle on the design and reproduce the motif in mirror image on the other side (2).

Symmetrical reproduction on one side

The same technique is used to reproduce a motif or design symmetrically on one side. The mirror can be adjusted until the best position is found (1) and a line ruled to mark its position on the paper. The design can now be transferred to the fabric and then reproduced in mirror image on the other side of the line (2).

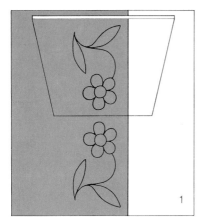

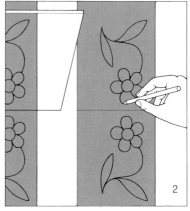

BASIC STITCHES FOR STARTING AND FASTENING OFF

In this chapter you will find explanations of some of the techniques and stitches which, although not always the main part of the embroidery, can often make or mar the final result. A good piece of needlework is always better if it has a suitable border or a neat hem and, if buttonholes or loops are necessary, they should be well made.

Overcasting and whipstitching are particularly useful basic stitches, one of their uses being in the setting up of a square embroidery frame. All the stitches described in this section are often important, too, as the basis for decorative stitches. A row of backstitching expertly worked, for instance, will make an excellent foundation for certain types of embroidery and ensure a more professional finish.

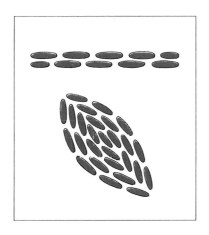

Running stitch

This is worked from right to left, picking up the same number of threads each time. If the fabric is fine, several stitches can be made before the thread is pulled through.

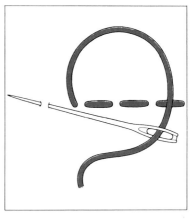

Padding stitch

This is used as a base for several stitches, both to outline the work and to make it stand out. When the decorative stitches are to be worked in a fairly short vertical or horizontal line, it is only necessary to lay a padding thread along the line to be worked, just catching it into the fabric at each end. When the line is fairly long or irregular the padding will consist of running stitches or basting (see page 40) over the areas to be embroidered.

Basting or Tacking

This is worked like running stitch (see page 39) except that the stitches should be alternately long and short.

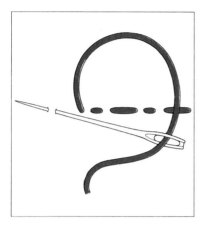

Backstitch

Working from right to left, bring the needle through to the right side of the fabric and make a small stitch backwards (towards the right).

Count the number of threads covered by this stitch and bring the needle through again in front of it the same number of threads forward. Take the needle through again into the front of the first stitch and repeat the process, always covering the same number of threads with each stitch. If the fabric is very fine, draw a thread (see page 53) and work on the opened row which will be covered by the backstitching.

Overcasting

This is a method sometimes used to prevent a raw edge from fraying. Bring the needle through to the right side of the fabric about 3–4 threads in from the edge. Repeat this operation, moving diagonally 3–4 threads to the left. The stitches must be evenly spaced and of a regular tension which allows the stitches to lie flat without curling the edge.

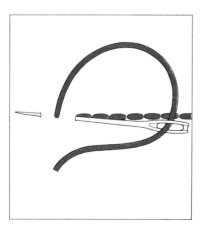

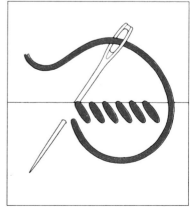

Whipstitching

There are two techniques involved in whipstitching, according to whether or not the two edges to be joined are selvedges. In dealing with sel-

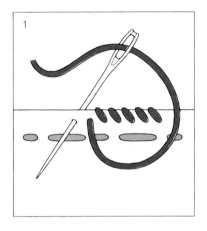

vedges, place the two edges together and baste (see opposite page) so that they will remain in position while the whipstitching is done. Now bring the needle through from the back of the fabric, about

2–3 threads from the edge of the selvedge, carry needle to back of fabric and bring through again diagonally a little way to the left (1). Continue in the same way until entire length has been joined. Remove basting stitches, open up the two pieces of fabric and press well under a damp cloth.

If the pieces to be joined have no selvedges, draw a thread (see page 53) to get the straight grain of the fabric and turn both edges in towards the back of the fabric for about $\frac{1}{4}$ in ($\frac{1}{2}$ cm). Place the two pieces flat, so that the prepared edges meet, and whipstitch together, bringing the needle diagonally through from the back, about 2–3 threads from the folded edge of one piece of fabric and then of the other, as shown in the diagram (2).

Straight overcast stitch

This makes a very neat edge to a border on fine fabric. A round, well twisted padding thread should always be laid along the edge first. Working from left to right, keep the

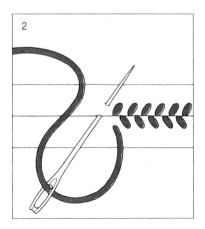

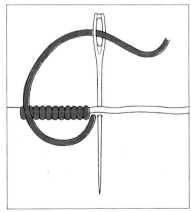

needle in a vertical position and insert it 2 threads from the edge, bringing it through again 1 thread further along horizontally. This will produce a firm, slightly corded effect.

Basic buttonhole stitch

First of all, fold the edge over for about $\frac{1}{4}$ in ($\frac{1}{2}$ cm). Working from left to right, insert the needle through from the right side of work, just below the folded edge, and bring out on the wrong side; take the needle through again from the right side, with the thread under the needle, to form a loop; pull the thread tight without puckering the fabric. Continue in this way, making the stitches very regular and as close to each other as possible, to the end.

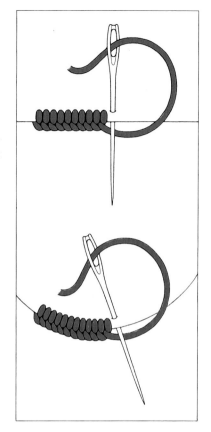

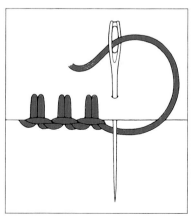

Double blanket stitch

First of all, fold the edge over for about $\frac{1}{4}$ in ($\frac{1}{2}$ cm). Working from left to right, insert the needle through to the back of the work and make the first stitch as for basic buttonhole stitch (see opposite page). Bring the needle through from the front to the back again, 2 threads diagonally towards the right thus moving 4 threads further along, taking the embroidery thread behind the eye of the needle and then under the point to form a second loop. Continue in this way to the end.

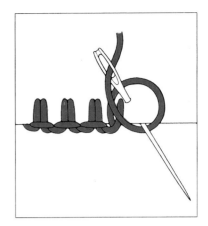

Buttonhole stitch with a double or triple twist

These variations are worked like the basic buttonhole stitch (see opposite page) except that, having inserted the needle through to the wrong side of the fabric, the thread is wound 2 or 3 times round its point, as shown in the diagrams.

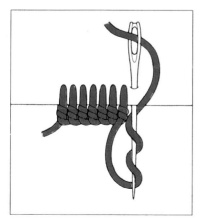

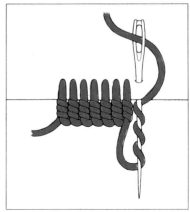

Diagonal buttonhole or blanket stitch

The method of execution is the same as for basic buttonhole stitch (see page 42), though the stitches are farther apart (see diagram below). Having folded the edge of the fabric over by $\frac{1}{4}$ in ($\frac{1}{2}$ cm), the stitches are worked over 10, 12, 14, 16, 14, 12, 10 vertical threads, using one straight and one diagonal stitch.

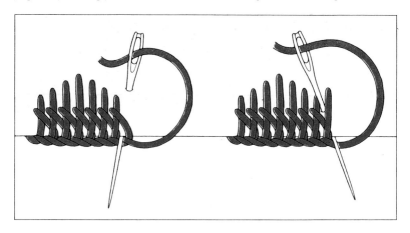

Blanket stitch used to join two pieces of fabric together

This stitch is most decorative. Having turned in the edges of both pieces of fabric to be joined, work one straight buttonhole stitch (see page 42) on one of them and then on the other, with a space of 4 threads between alternate stitches.

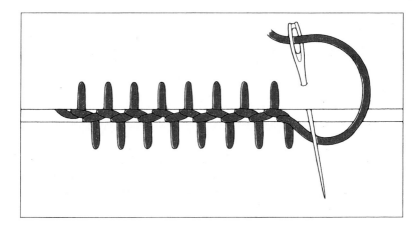

Paris stitch

Working from right to left, take up 3–4 threads of the fabric horizontally and fasten with a backstitch (see page 40). Bring the needle out diagonally, to the right side of work, 3–4 threads to the left and 4 threads above the horizontal stitch already worked. Work another horizontal backstitch in line with the first one and continue in the same way.

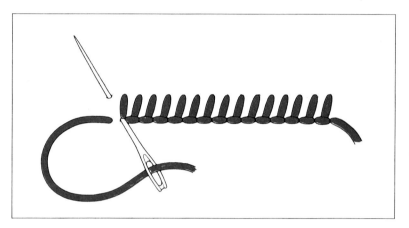

Simple hemstitch on drawn-thread work or single openwork

This is worked on fabric with an even weave whose threads are easy to count and to withdraw (see page 53). Working from the back, from left to right, pass the needle from right to left under 3 threads, draw it out, and pass it from below upwards under 2 threads of the fabric.

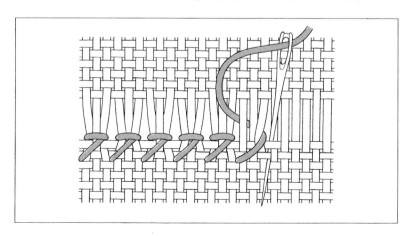

Double or treble hemstitch

This is worked on fabric prepared as follows: 3 threads withdrawn, 2 left, 3 threads withdrawn, etc. Simple hemstitching (see page 45) is then worked over each pair of horizontal threads, as illustrated.

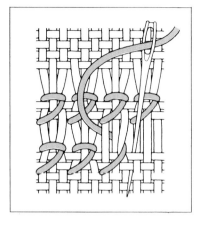

Ladder hemstitch

Having withdrawn 3 or more threads from the fabric, work in simple hemstitching (see page 45) along one side then turn and work another row along the other side, keeping the threads grouped as before.

Serpentine or trellis hemstitch

Having withdrawn at least 3 threads from the fabric, work in simple hemstitching (see page 45) but taking up an even number of threads each time. When the row is complete, turn and work the first stitch by taking up only half the threads in the first group, after which each group will be formed from half of each of two groups to form a zig-zag line.

Simple four-sided stitch

In order to work this stitch, which is executed on the right side of the fabric, some threads have to be withdrawn first (see page 53). Draw 1 thread out, leave 4 and draw another 1 out. The stitch is then worked, as shown in the diagram, from number 1 to number 7, always starting the next stitch from number 2. The horizontal stitches are taken over 4 threads of the fabric.

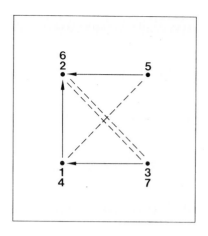

Double four-sided stitch

Worked in the same way as the simple four-sided stitch (see above), except that each side is doubled. Withdraw threads as for the simple stitch and then follow the diagram from number 1 to number 13, always starting the next stitch from number 2. As before, the horizontal stitches are taken over 4 threads of the fabric.

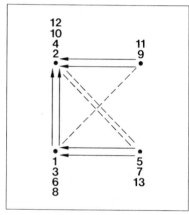

Turkish stitch

Withdraw threads as follows: draw 1 thread out, leave 4 and draw another 1 out. This stitch is worked on the right side of the fabric and each stitch is doubled. Follow the diagram from number 1 to number 17, always starting the next stitch from number 2. The horizontal stitches are taken over 6 threads of the fabric and each diagonal stitch covers 3 threads.

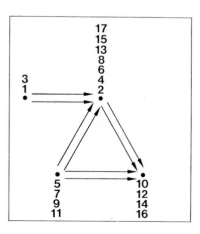

Up-and-down stitch

Withdraw threads as follows: draw 1 thread, leave 4, draw 4 threads, leave 4, draw 1 thread. The stitch is worked vertically, from top to bottom, on the right side of the fabric and consists of two main parts as shown in the diagram. For the first part, work over 2 threads only and follow the top section of the diagram by bringing the needle through to the right side at number 1 and continuing to number 7. Now repeat the stitches from 2 to 7.

For the second part, finish withdrawing the threads as indicated above and work as shown in the second section of the diagram, bringing the needle through at number 1 and continuing to number 14. Now repeat the stitches from 2 to 14.

Isolated overcast bars

Withdraw the requisite number of horizontal threads, and hemstitch each side, if the fabric is likely to fray. Start by carrying the embroidery thread down the first column of 4 threads so that it is anchored as you work up it in straight overcast stitch (see page 41), keeping the stitches close together. Continue in this way, working down one group of 4 threads and up the next to the end.

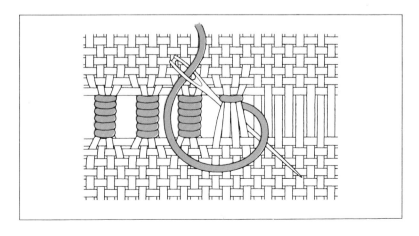

48

Drawn threads for darned bars

Darned bars are simple to work. At least 20 threads should be drawn, releasing vertical threads, which must be divisible by 6 or 9, over the area required, and the two side edges hemstitched in one of the variations already described (see pages 45–6).

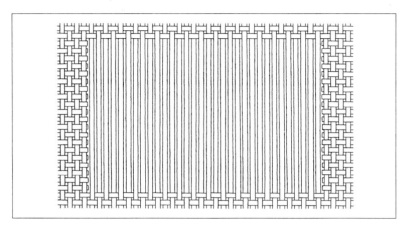

Darned bars

Bring needle through to right side of work in the lower left corner of drawn work. Take it over the first 3 threads, under the next 3 and tighten the thread. Repeat the same operation in the other direction, taking the needle over the 3 threads on the right and under the 3 threads on the left. Continue, working first from the bottom and then from the top.

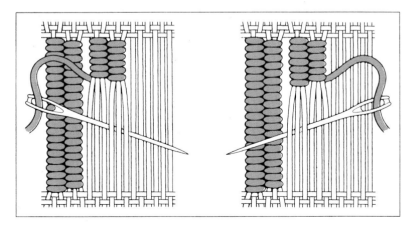

Triple darned bars

In this case, the number of vertical bars must be divisible by 9. Start as for the ordinary darned bars taking the needle over the first 3 threads, under the next 3 and over the next 3. On the return, take the needle under the 3 threads on the right, over the 3 middle ones and under the 3 on the left. Continue, working first from the bottom and then from the top.

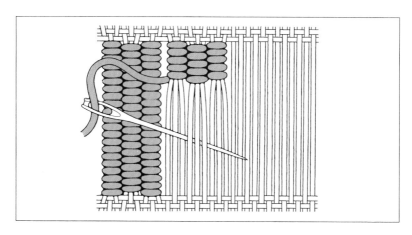

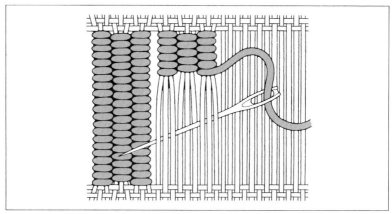

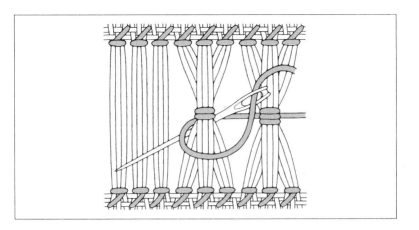

Openwork strip with one row of clusters

Withdraw at least 20 threads to leave a number of vertical threads divisible by 6. Work ladder hemstitching (see page 46), then fasten on a working thread in the middle of the first three groups of 2 threads on the right. Pass it around all 6 threads three times and, at the third turn, pass the needle under the first two turns, at the back, to secure the thread. Continue in this way to the end.

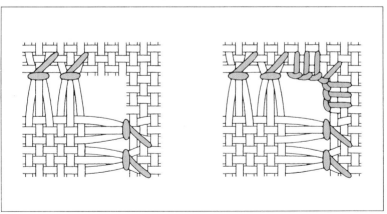

Finishing off a hemstitched corner

Having withdrawn the necessary threads, including the corner (see page 54), hemstitch along one side and, when the corner is reached, work in basic buttonhole stitch (see page 42) as shown in the diagram. Continue hemstitching along next side and repeat process at each corner.

Finishing off a hemstitched corner with crossed bars

Withdraw the threads for the corner as described on page 54. When one row of ladder hemstitching (see page 46) is complete, cover the last group of 2 threads with basic buttonhole stitch (see page 42), then the first group in the next row and the other two sides of the square, taking up 3 threads of the fabric. To reinforce the corner and add further decoration, when the buttonholing is complete, take the embroidery thread diagonally from one corner to another to form an "X" and cover with straight overcasting (see page 41).

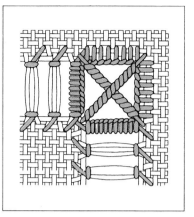

Woven spider's web corners worked into single rows of clusters

Having worked the single row of clusters, take the central working thread to the opposite side of the corner square and do the same thing with the central working thread from the row coming in at a right angle (1). Now take a thread to each corner of the square (2). Fasten the

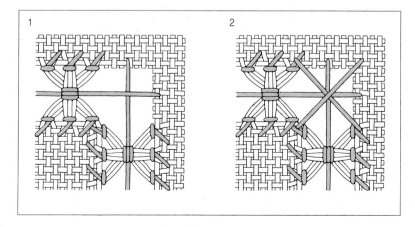

working thread to the point at which all the threads cross and weave it over and under each spoke until a small web has been formed (3). Cover all the spokes and the two raw edges of the fabric with straight overcasting (see page 41) or basic buttonhole stitch (see page 42).

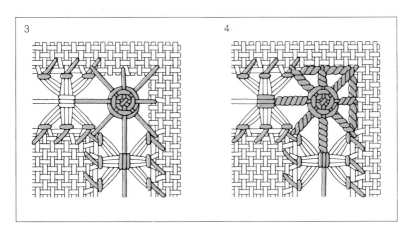

Cutting on the straight grain and drawing threads

Fabric used for embroidery, unless deliberately cut on the cross or in a circular shape, is generally square or

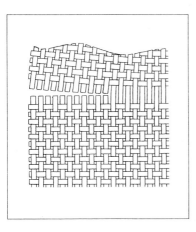

rectangular. In this case, it is always cut on the straight grain, the sides being completely perpendicular. To ensure that the fabric is, in fact, on the straight grain simply withdraw a thread or, if the fabric is very fine, 2 threads a few millimeters from the edge of each side. Any excess fabric can then be cut away, following the line left by the drawn threads.

Many embroidery stitches necessitate the withdrawal of threads from the fabric so that decoration can be worked on the threads thus released. The effect of such openwork is very striking. Threads can be withdrawn either vertically or horizontally, that is to say, both the warp and the weft can be involved. In either case, the threads must be cut with great precision at the points from where they are to be withdrawn; they can then be carefully pulled out, one at a time, with the aid of a needle.

Corners and insertions in drawn-thread work

When threads have been withdrawn both horizontally and vertically, the resulting corners will be as shown in diagram (1).

Sometimes threads have to be withdrawn from a specific area of the fabric and not from the whole length of the warp and weft. In this case, about $\frac{1}{2}$ in (1 cm) of each cut thread should be left free at both ends of the work (2). These can be secured later by working straight overcasting (see

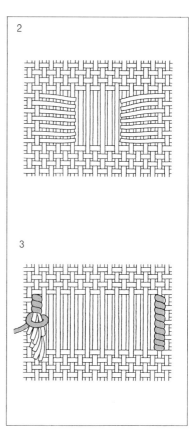

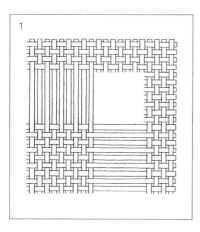

page 41) or basic buttonholing (see page 42) over 2 or 3 threads of the fabric and covering them at the same time (3).

Making a hem – blind-stitching

Before starting this operation, make sure that the fabric is cut perfectly on the straight grain (see page 53). Now turn up about $\frac{1}{4}$ in ($\frac{1}{2}$ cm) on all sides of the fabric, making the fold by pressing along it with the thumb-

nail. Having decided the required depth of hem, turn the fabric up again to this width and baste (see page 40) into position about $\frac{1}{10}$ in (2–3 mm) from the turned in edge. If no decorative stitches are to be used on the hem, blind-stitching is normally used to hold it in place as this is not visible on the right side. It is worked as follows: take the needle through to the right side of the fabric, about a thread's distance from the folded edge, and bring it back diagonally, to the left, 2 threads

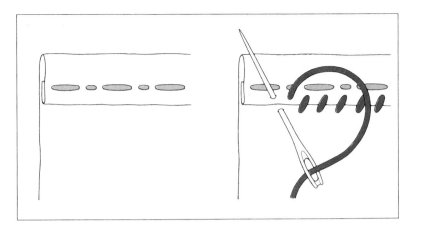

away from the fold. Continue in this way along the entire length of the hem. The result will be a row of small diagonal stitches on the wrong side with 2–3 of the fabric's threads between each one. Remove basting.

Hemming the corners

To hem the corners, fold the point inwards for the same width as the hem you require plus $\frac{1}{4}$ in ($\frac{1}{2}$ cm). Cut away to $\frac{1}{4}$ in ($\frac{1}{2}$ cm) from the fold and complete the hem on each side with blind-stitching, as just described. Now finish off the corner seam with flat whipstitching (see page 41).

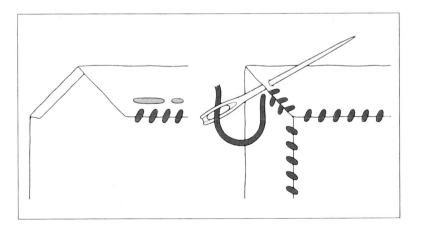

Binding a hem

Seam binding can be used to finish off an edge. This should first be backstitched (see page 40) neatly into position along the edge of the right side of the work. Press flat under a damp cloth. Now turn binding onto the wrong side of the work and work along its edge in either back- or blind-stitching (see page 54). To give body to this type of

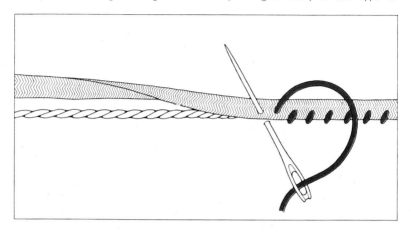

hem, a length of piping cord can be inserted while the second edge of the binding is being sewn.

Buttonholes

There is only one basic way to make hand-worked buttonholes, with two slight variations which depend on the thickness of the fabric. Working

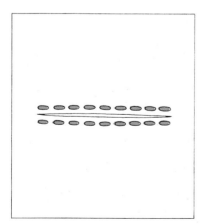

on the right side of the cloth, mark the positions of the buttonholes in chalk or with a long stitch, the size being very slightly larger (about $\frac{1}{8}$ in or 3 mm) than that of the buttons and larger still if these are very thick. Cut along the marked line and reinforce the edges by working a row of very small running stitches (see page 39) along both sides. Now work in basic buttonhole stitch (see page 42) but, if the fabric is fine, when one side of the buttonhole has been completed, make 3 vertical stitches at the end, turn the work and complete the other side (1). If the fabric is thick, instead of working straight stitches at the end of the first side, continue in buttonhole stitch which will fan out slightly as you turn the work to complete the second side (2).

Button loops

The size of button loops is governed by the size of the buttons. Loops may be worked either on the edge or on the main body of the fabric but the method is the same in either case.

Bring the thread through to the right side of the work and carry it over to the right, leaving it slack enough to form the size of loop required. Repeat this operation back and forth 3 or 4 times and then cover all the strands in basic buttonhole stitch (see page 42) worked very close together. Such loops can also be used, in different sizes, for hanging up tea towels, hand towels, articles of clothing, etc.

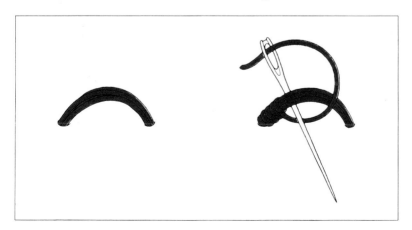

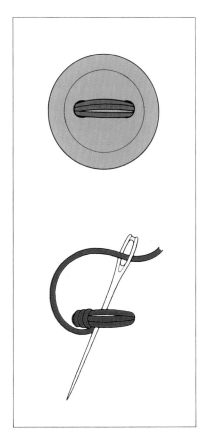

Sewing on buttons

Fasten the thread securely at the point where the button is required and bring the needle up through one of the holes in the button and then insert it down through the other to the back of the work, leaving a short length between the button and the fabric. Repeat this process 4 or 5 times, making sure that the needle always goes in and comes out at the same point on the wrong side. If the button has four holes, repeat the operation through the other two holes. Turn to the back of the work and neaten the stitches by working a few straight overcasting stitches (see page 41) over them. Now bring the needle back to the right side again, under the button and close to the holes; wind the thread several times around the base of the button to form a shank. Fasten securely by taking the needle through one side of the shank, take through to the back and cut the thread with small, sharp scissors.

The best types of thread to use for sewing on buttons are those of which the fabric is made, i.e. cotton on cotton, man-made threads on polyester and nylon. For heavy garments, however, linen thread rubbed over beeswax is ideal.

78 stitches: instructions for every type of embroidery

Stem stitch

This is certainly the best known and most used of all the stitches. Although it is easy to work, precision is essential to produce a really good result. It is used mainly to define lines and outlines but can also be used as a filling in stitch if the rows are kept close together. It stands out well on any type of fabric and in any type of thread, providing this is appropriate to the fabric.

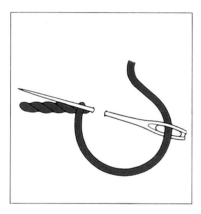

Basic stem stitch

Having secured the thread firmly on the wrong side of the fabric, bring the needle through to the right side and pick up a few threads of fabric horizontally, keeping the working thread looped either below the needle or above it. The needle should be pointing towards the left although the stitch is worked from left to right. Pull the working thread through and insert the needle again on the line to be covered and bring it through at the end of the stitch just worked. Continue in this way, without changing the position of the working thread. This is important because by keeping it below the needle, the stitches will slope towards the left and conversely by keeping it above the needle, the stitches will slope towards the right.

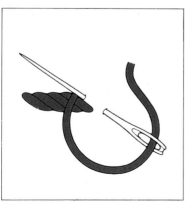

Encroaching stem stitch

This is worked in the same way as basic stem stitch except that the needle is brought up half-way along the length of the previous stitch.

Split stem stitch

This is worked in the same way as encroaching stem stitch except that the needle is brought up through the strands of the previous stitch, splitting it in half.

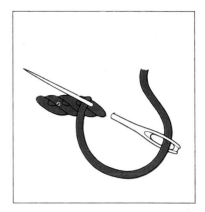

Chain stitch

Chain stitch is one of the basic embroidery stitches and is particularly suitable for defining lines and outlines as well as rounded and spiral designs. It can also be used as a filling and padding stitch by keeping the rows close together. Any type of thread may be used providing it is appropriate to the fabric.

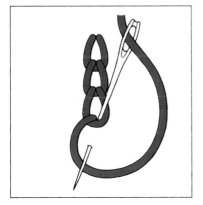

Basic chain stitch

Bring the needle through to the right side of work. Keeping the thread under the left thumb, take the needle down vertically through the fabric exactly where the thread was brought from the back and pick up a few strands of fabric. Keeping the loop under the needle, bring the needle out on the right side and draw the thread through.

Still keeping the thread for the next stitch under the left thumb, insert the needle down vertically through the loop formed by the preceding stitch and, keeping the loop under the needle, bring it out again on right side of work, drawing the thread through.

Continue in the same way, being careful to keep the stitches the same length and following closely the line of the design. These stitches will appear as an even row of backstitches on the reverse of the work.

Chain stitches should always be kept rather loose, especially when working a curved line.

Whipped chain stitch

Start by working the basic chain stitch as required by design. Turn work round and, working from right to left, work a whipstitch (see page 41) over each chain stitch by bringing the needle over one stitch and diagonally under the next one. Take care not to pick up any of the fabric.

This is particularly effective if the whipping thread is in a contrasting color to that used for the chain.

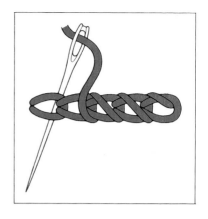

Twisted chain stitch

This is worked as for basic chain stitch (see page 61) except that instead of taking the needle through the middle of the preceding stitch it is taken through to the left of it, crossing the thread over as shown in the illustration.

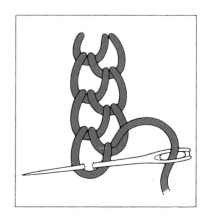

Double chain stitch

Work as for basic chain stitch (see page 61), making first one stitch to the left and then one to the right. The right-hand stitch must be worked slightly below the left-hand one so that the two linked rows of chain are staggered.

Feathered chain stitch

This is primarily a border stitch and is worked as for basic chain stitch except that each chain is worked alternately to the left and right, each one being joined by a short straight stitch, as shown in the illustration. This stitch is easier to work if the fabric is held on the cross and the fabric marked up with parallel guide-lines to keep the width even. The evenness and regular slant of the stitches are important to the attractiveness of this variation.

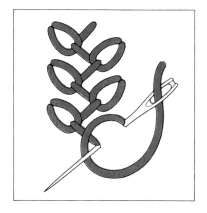

Feather stitch

A stitch that may be used for filling or for stems and borders. It is suitable for working on any type of fabric providing an appropriate thread is used.

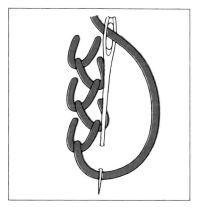

Basic feather stitch

Bring needle through to right side of work and, keeping the thread over to the left-hand side, take a vertical stitch and bring needle through to right side, just above the thread held on the left to form a loop. Now take the needle to the right of the emerging thread (as shown in illustration), still keeping the thread to the left, and make another stitch as before, bringing the needle out over the thread on the left. Now take the needle to the left of the emerging thread and, this time, bring the thread over to the right; make a stitch, bringing the needle out over the thread.

Each stitch will produce a "U" shaped loop, alternating between left and right. On the back of the work, there will be two parallel rows of alternating running stitches.

Slanting feather stitch

This is worked as for basic feather stitch (see page 63) except that the needle is slanted to the left and right on alternate stitches.

Double feather stitch

This is worked as for basic feather stitch (see page 63) except that two stitches are made to the right and two to the left. Variations can be worked by increasing the number of stitches on each side.

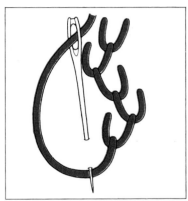

Closed feather stitch

This is worked as for basic feather stitch (see page 63) except that the needle is held vertically rather than diagonally, the stitches being taken alternately to the right and left of the start of the preceding stitch so that an almost unbroken line is formed at the outer edges of the stitches.

Lazy daisy stitch

This is also known as "Detached chain stitch." It is easy to work and is very effective, usually used for the petals of flowers and the edges of leaves. When spaced out individually, the stitch gives an attractive speckled effect. All the variations can be worked on any type of fabric, providing an appropriate thread is used.

Basic lazy daisy stitch or detached chain stitch

Bring thread through to right side of fabric and work a simple chain stitch (see page 61), anchoring it with a small stitch taken over the end of the loop. The needle will now be on the wrong side of the work again and a new stitch can be made either close to the first one, to start forming a flower, or at random if a speckled effect is required.

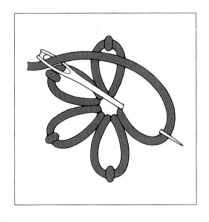

Threaded chain stitch

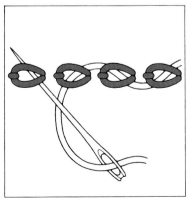

Work a row of lazy daisy stitches, about $\frac{1}{4}$ in ($\frac{1}{2}$ cm), either vertically or horizontally, and finish off. Now, working from right to left, bring thread through to right side of work and weave it under each stitch, threading it alternately upwards and downwards. Care must be taken not to penetrate the fabric and to keep the thread at the same tension throughout this operation. A thread of contrasting color and/or texture can be most effective.

Knotted stitches

Knotted stitches are suitable for lines, outlines and filling. They can be worked on any fabric in appropriate threads.

Basic knot stitch

Bring thread through to right side of work, keeping needle pointing horizontally from right to left and the working thread over the needle to the right. Working vertically, leave a small space from where thread emerges and pick up an amount of fabric twice as long as the space just left; carry working thread around the needle from right to left, as in the illustration, and pull the thread while, at the same time, centering the knot that has been made. Leave another space, as before, still traveling vertically and, with the needle pointing horizontally from right to left, pick up a piece of fabric twice as long as the space just left; carry working thread around the needle and pull the thread through. Continue in this way, as required by the design.

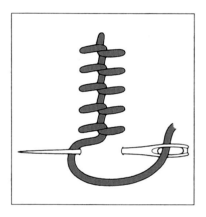

Spanish knot stitch

Bring thread through to right side of fabric and, working vertically, leave a small space before picking up a piece of fabric half the width of the space just left, keeping the thread to the right. Keeping a loop upwards, position the needle as shown in the illustration and pull the thread through. Pull out the last stitch a little with the point of the needle to form a loop and continue in the same way, as the design requires.

Coral stitch

Bring thread through to right side of fabric and, working vertically, leave a small space before inserting the needle to the right at an angle, keeping the working thread upwards, and pull through. Now position the needle to point from left to right under the slanting stitch and pull thread through. Work another slanting stitch to the right and continue in the same way.

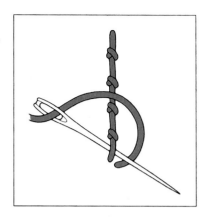

Branch stitch

This stitch is mainly used for wider borders and as a filling. It is not one of the simplest of stitches to work as the greatest possible precision is essential. It may be worked with any thread on appropriate fabric.

Bring thread through to right side of fabric and, holding it down with the left thumb, position the needle to point horizontally to the right and pass through to the back, having left a small space. Still at the back

of the work, position the needle horizontally towards the left and bring it through to the front half way along the horizontal stitch just worked, and anchor the loop down with a small vertical stitch. The needle will now be at the back again.

Bring thread through exactly below the start of the first stitch and work as explained. It is most important for all the stitches to be aligned vertically and for their length and tension to be exactly the same throughout the design.

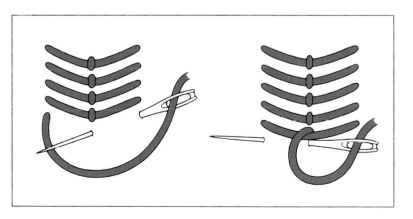

Matting stitch

This is a stitch that is used a great deal for covering quite large areas. It is suitable for any type of fabric providing an appropriate thread is used. By varying the angle of the blocks of stitches, very interesting effects of light and shadow can be achieved.

Make a long stitch from one side of the space to be filled to the other – either from bottom to top or from right to left. Now bring the needle out at about the fourth fabric thread below the top of the long stitch, keeping the working thread to the left, and pull through. Working towards the start of the long stitch, work small slanting stitches over it, catching up a little piece of fabric underneath with each stitch. When the whole of the long stitch has been covered, make another long stitch very close to it and cover it in the same way. Repeat as required until the outline has been completely filled.

Bokhara couching

This is one of the most widely used embroidery stitches especially for covering large areas of fabric. It can be used on any type of fabric with an appropriate thread, although the best results are obtained with pearl cotton, (coton perlé), which accentuates the effect of shading which is characteristic of this stitch.

Make a long stitch from the lower edge of space to be filled to the top or from side to side. bring needle out at a point about 2 strands of fabric below the top of the stitch and then work back towards the start of the long stitch by anchoring it down with evenly spaced small, slanting stitches. Now make another long stitch at a little distance to the left of the first and repeat the process. Continue until whole outline has been filled in.

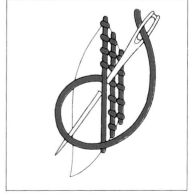

Buttonhole scalloping

This may be used as an edging or for internal ornamentation and the basis for those two very decorative types of embroidery, guipure and Richelieu. It is generally worked on fabric that does not fray, such as cotton, as it is so often used on the edges of cut-out embroidery. The most suitable embroidery thread is a buttonhole twist in an appropriate thickness for the fabric being used. It is not difficult to do but, to be effective, it must be worked with great precision.

It is necessary first to prepare the base on which the design will be worked by putting a row of running stitches along all the outlines (see page 39). If the area to be covered is small enough, this will provide sufficient thickness for the embroidery. If quite large surfaces are to be covered, the spaces between the outlines should be filled in with rows of backstitching worked backwards and forwards (see page 40). Another type of padding can be used in the form of a narrow piping cord which is caught up with the fabric as the buttonholing is worked.

To work the stitch, bring the needle through on right side of fabric and, holding it vertically downwards, take up a few strands of fabric as defined by the outline of running stitches. Take the working thread under the point of the needle, holding it with the left thumb, and pull thread through. A small loop is thus formed. The next and following stitches are worked in the same way keeping them very close together and of equal tension.

If the work has to be cut, use small, sharp and well pointed embroidery scissors to remove the necessary pieces of fabric. Keep as close as possible to the stitches but be very careful not to cut them.

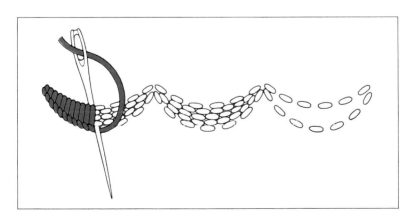

Croatian stitch

This stitch is a traditional one, being used particularly in national Croatian dress. It shows up to best advantage when worked in a color that contrasts strongly with the fabric or when a different color is used for each stage of the stitch itself. A rather thick embroidery thread gives a particularly striking effect. Croatian stitch is not suitable for covering large areas.

Work a row of running stitch (see page 39) over the outline, taking care that all the stitches are the same length and tension. When this has been completed, either continue with the same thread or change to another color. If you decide on a contrast, finish off the used thread on the wrong side and bring the new one through to the right side. Now fill in the background by taking the working thread under a running stitch on alternate sides of the design without picking up any fabric threads. When complete, take thread through to back of work and finish off by working into the backs of a few of the running stitches.

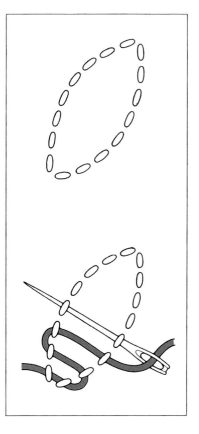

Satin stitch

Satin stitch is one of the most attractive embroidery stitches. It can be used for flowers and other decorative objects that rely on body rather than line for their effect. It is a stitch that gives considerable scope for shading. Satin stitch can be worked on any type of fabric, including fine ones such as silk. Any type of embroidery thread can be used to give varying effects, depending on the fabric.

A particularly elegant effect can be achieved by working this stitch in white on white fabric, giving a slightly iridescent appearance.

Long and short satin stitch and Encroaching satin stitch

Once the design has been transferred onto the fabric, work a few stitches near the central or focal point of the shape. Keeping the stitches close together, they should be alternately long and short. Continue in this way over the second half, returning by working long stitches below the short ones and short stitches below the long ones. Work in a similar way until the whole motif has been filled.

To achieve the effect of shading, a slight variation of technique can be used. This is known as "encroaching satin stitch" and is achieved by using a different shade of the same color as the first row (or a different color, when appropriate) and working the tops of the second and subsequent rows of stitches in between the bases of the stitches in the previous row. In this way, the colors will blend together without any hard lines forming. Always work towards the center and then out from it, as already described. Continue in this way, always starting the first stitch at its lowest point.

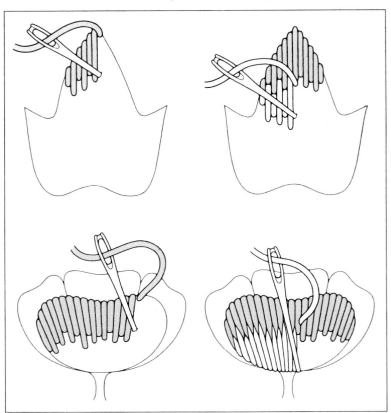

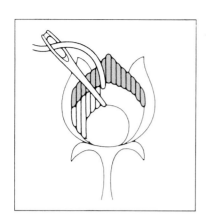

Chinese or Jacobean satin stitch

This is worked as described for the long and short satin stitch (see page 71), except that the bases of the first row of stitches form a defined line and all the shades or changes of color also remain within the "cells" indicated by the transferred design. The effect, although formal, is striking.

Broderie anglaise or Madeira work

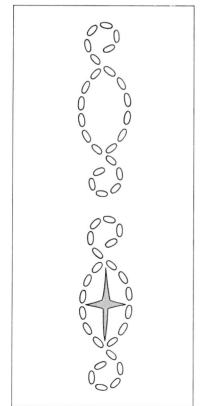

This is not exactly a stitch but a style of embroidery in which two or three basic stitches are involved to create dainty decorative embroidery to cover fairly large areas. It is usually found in embroidery on white materials, at one time worked in white thread only but nowadays in colored as well, and is therefore especially suitable for lingerie, bed linen and hand-towels. The technique originated in England in the early days of the cotton industry but it has had a new lease of life in recent years when it has become very popular as trimming on ladies' summer clothes and on bed linen. The new embroidery, however, frequently features colored thread on white fabric or white thread on colored fabric, which is often in such dark shades as black, navy blue, etc., in order to make the work stand out. The designs are usually geometric featuring lozenge shapes, triangles and very small eyelets which may even be made with a sewing stiletto or steel knitting needle.

When the design, which will consist of outlined shapes and some cutwork motifs, has been transferred onto the fabric, work a row of small running stitches (see page 39) over all the lines. The shapes to be out-lined can now be worked in straight overcasting (see page 41).

Those parts of the design to be embroidered in open-work can be carefully cut with small, sharp pointed scissors after they have been outlined with running stitches. In the case of the larger areas, cut the fabric at the center of the area to be opened in the form of a cross (see illust-ration) and turn the raw edges to back of work. Complete by working in straight overcasting all round, catching in raw edge and bringing needle through to the out-side edge of the running stitches each time.

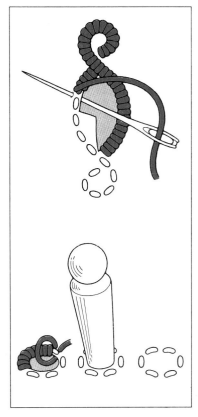

Straight stitch or Foundation stitch

This can be worked on any type of fabric in any appropriate thread. It may be used as a decorative stitch or as a basis for the buttonholed bars in guipure work.

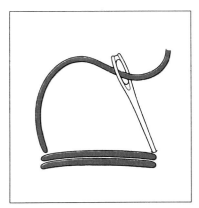

Bring the needle through to right side of work and, having made a stitch of up to 1–1½ in (3–4 cm), take needle back to wrong side. This is usually repeated about three times in a group, when used as a found-ation stitch. It is very important not to make the stitches tight as the work will pucker and be spoiled.

Palestrina stitch or Double knot stitch

This stitch is particularly characteristic of Italian embroidery and takes its name from a little town to the east of Rome. It is particularly suitable for lines, outlines and curved shapes and is worked by making a series of knots which can be spaced close together or far apart, according to the length of the stitches. It is a very decorative stitch and is most effective when worked in a rather thick embroidery thread such as pearl cotton (coton perlé) on a fairly heavy fabric.

Palestrina stitch can be worked downwards or sideways from left to right. Bring the thread through to right side of work and insert needle a little below and slightly to the right point of emergence and pick up a small piece of fabric, making a stitch on back of work. All three points of entry should be equidistant (top). Pull thread through and slip the needle through the bar already formed without picking up any fabric (center). Holding the thread down with the left thumb, slip the needle under the bar again below the last stitch and take it over the working thread rather as in blanket stitch (bottom).

Continue in the same way, taking care not to pull the thread too tight. On the back of the work there will be a row of equidistant parallel vertical stitches.

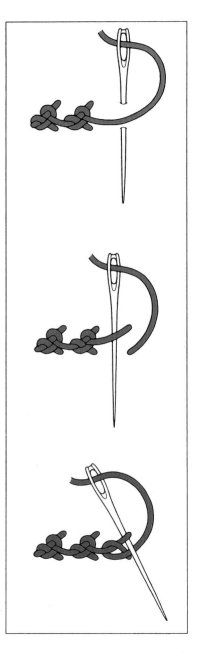

Herringbone stitch

This is a decorative version of the
"Catch stitch" used on hems in ordinary sewing. As a decorative stitch, it
is worked on counted threads on
rather fine fabrics with fine threads
and is particularly suitable for white
embroidery.

Background herringbone is especially useful for filling small areas
and is very easy to work.

Basic herringbone stitch

Working from left to right, bring
needle through to right side of work
at lower end of first stitch, take the
working thread diagonally to the
right, over the desired number of
threads. Insert the needle through to
the right side at a distance of 3 or 4
threads horizontally to the left of last
point of entry. Make another stitch
diagonally to the right of the same
length as the first and bring needle
out again 3 or 4 threads horizontally
to the left. Continue in this way,
taking care to keep the stitches even.
Turn work at end of each row to
maintain direction.

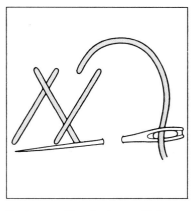

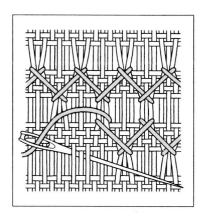

Background herringbone stitch

Prepare the fabric by drawing some
threads (see page 53); the proportion of drawn threads to those remaining depends largely on the type
of weave but a suggestion would be
3 drawn to 4 undrawn. The stitch is
then worked, as already explained
for basic herringbone, over the undrawn threads. Turn work at end of
each row to maintain direction.

Padded satin stitch

This is worked in the same way as basic satin stitch (see page 77), except that it is "padded' with stitches first to give extra body to the shapes, giving them a raised effect. Even greater precision is necessary than in working basic satin stitch as any imperfections are immediately apparent, such as puckering, badly defined outlines and an irregular surface. It is advisable to use an embroidery frame when working this stitch.

Having transferred the design to the fabric, work a row of small running stitches (see page 39) along all the outlines. Now fill in the spaces with rows of alternating running stitches until the surface of every part of each motif is completely padded.

Finally, working from left to right, make a row of vertical stitches right over the padding. These stitches must be kept close together with the needle being used in a downward direction all the time.

When only small areas have to be filled, mark the outlines with running stitches, as already described, and fill with basic satin stitch (see page 77) worked horizontally. Complete by working the top stitches vertically, as explained above.

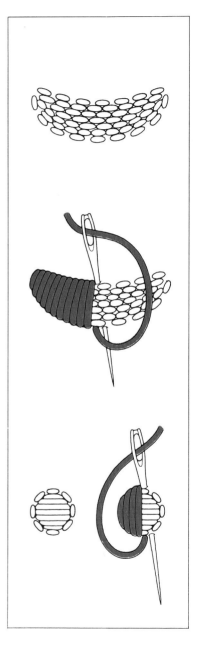

Woven stitch

This is a useful stitch for covering large areas, creating the effect of the warp and weft of weaving. Interesting results can be achieved by using contrasting colors or different shades of one color in the two stages of the work.

Start by working vertical stitches, close together, right over the area to be covered. Now, either with the same thread or one of a different color, starting from the top work a small stitch over the center stitch then, keeping the rows close together, weave across from left to right and right to left, inserting the working thread through to the back of the fabric at the end of each row and bringing it through to the front again, in position to start the next row.

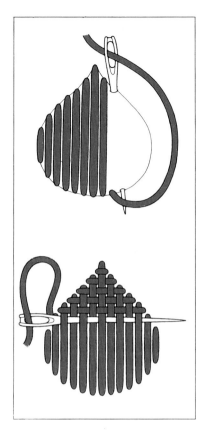

Vertical satin stitch

This stitch is suitable as a filling for fairly small areas and can be worked on ordinary fabrics or on evenly woven fabrics and canvases such as those used for counted-thread embroidery. The working thread must be appropriate to the weight of the fabric and cover it well, to give a solid effect. It should also be remembered that all the stitches must be accurately worked in order to achieve a smooth, satiny appearance; the edge of the design must be

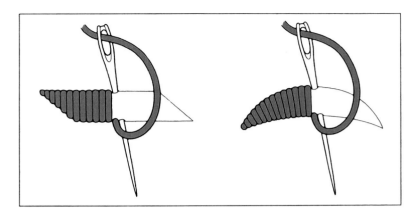

well defined and even, the stitches close together and the tension regular. It is advisable to use an embroidery frame.

Once the design has been transferred to the fabric, work from left to right and fill the spaces by making vertical stitches, very close together. Starting at the bottom of the left hand point, bring the needle through to the front and insert the needle on the opposite side of the design, as shown in the illustration on the left.

When working curves, the stitches should be somewhat closer together as curved lines get narrower, although no overlapping must be visible.

Holbein or Double running stitch

All the versions of this stitch should be worked on evenly woven fabrics such as those used for counted-thread embroidery. It is worked in two stages; the design is first outlined in running stitches and then gone over again, completing the line or design with further running stitches of exactly the same size as the first. Recommended threads are either pearl cotton (coton perlé) or soft embroidery thread.

Holbein or Double running stitch for outlining

Work a row of running stitches (see page 39) from right to left, turn the work and fill in the gaps between the stitches with another series of running stitches. This will produce a single line although worked in two directions.

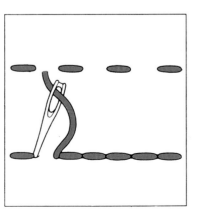

Stepped Holbein stitch

The first stage consists of running stitches (see page 39) worked vertically from left to right; each stitch is started on a level with the top of the stitch just worked and the distance between is the same as the length of the stitches. On the return journey, work horizontal running stitches from right to left between each stitch previously worked to give the effect of steps.

Zig-zag Holbein stitch

Going from left to right, the first row is worked in slanting running stitches (see page 39) of equal height and distance. On the return journey, which is worked from right to left, these are joined by another series of running stitches slanting in the opposite direction.

Shadow stitch (also known as Crossed or Double backstitch)

This stitch is usually worked on fine or semi-transparent fabrics as it gives a shadowy effect on the right side which emphasizes the transparency of the fabric itself. Soft embroidery cotton in very delicate shades is usually used.

Designs to be worked in shadow stitch are drawn on the wrong side of the fabric and often consist of two parallel lines. If an embroidery frame is used, the stitch is worked on the right side but if, as is usually the case, no frame is used, it is worked from the back of the fabric. The method given here is from the back.

Having transferred the design onto the back of the fabric, bring the needle through and begin to work the crossed stitching as shown in the illustration at the top of page 80. You will thus have crossed stitches on the back (top) and two rows of small stitches joined together on the front which clearly define the outline of the design (bottom). It should be remembered that the stitches will have to be slightly closer together as curved lines get narrower and farther apart as they widen out. An even tension of the thread must be maintained to avoid puckering.

French knot

This stitch may be worked on any type of fabric with any appropriate thread. There is no need for a detailed design as the knots can be used to give interest in many ways. They can be sprinkled over fairly large areas to give a powdered look or, in smaller spaces, may be worked close together to produce a textured effect. They are frequently used for flower pistils.

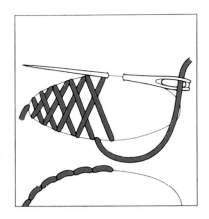

Pick up 2 or 3 threads of the fabric with the needle as close as you can to the point where the working thread emerges. While keeping the thread taught and close to the fabric with the thumb and forefinger of the left hand, twist it two or three times around the needle. Pull the thread through, at the same time keeping the knot in position with the left hand. Now turn the needle completely and insert it close to the start of the stitch, thus completing it. To make the next knot, bring the needle through at the desired point and repeat the process.

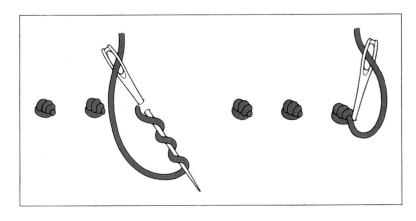

Algerian eye stitch

Algerian eye stitch can be worked on
evenly woven fabrics or on single or
double mesh canvas in stranded or
pearl cotton (coton perlé). If the
fabric is suitable, tapestry wool may
also be used. On canvas, this stitch is
usually worked to cover the background completely. Each "star" may
be used as an isolated motif or,
alternatively, worked in groups,
joined together or even superim-
posed on each other.

Separate Algerian eye stitch

Bring the needle through to right
side of work at the point marking the
outer tip of left horizontal point of
the star, insert it down through the
center and bring it out again diagonally to the left; insert it back
through the center and bring it out
vertically at the bottom of the next
point; take it back through the center
and continue in this way until eight
points have been made. Always
work in an anticlockwise direction,
bringing the needle through the center with each stitch, all of which
must be of equal length. If the fabric
is not suitable for counted thread
work, it is advisable to draw the stars
on it, as accurately as possible,
before starting the embroidery.

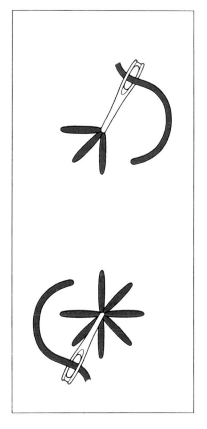

Continuous Algerian eye stitch

This is worked in two phases, first from left to right and then from right to left. The upper points of each star in the row are worked in the first phase and the lower points in the second. The illustrations show how the thread travels in both phases.

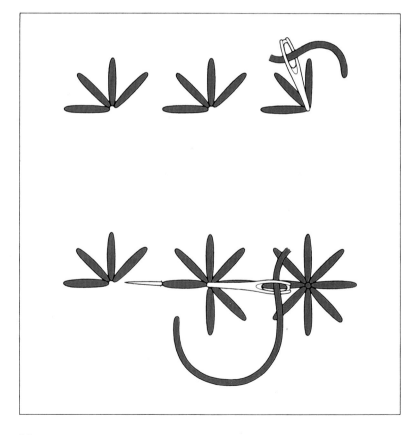

Faggot stitch – single or two-sided square Holbein stitch

This stitch is worked on delicate fabrics in fine thread to give the effect of drawn-thread work on small strips of fabric. It is usually combined with Shadow stitch (see page 79).

The stitches are worked in two stages, back and forth, starting from the top right and working diagonally down to the left. This forms squares on the front of the work and rows of diagonal stitches on the back.

Bring the needle through to front and make a horizontal stitch to the right over 3 or 4 threads (1–2). Bring needle through at a point to the left, just below the beginning of the first stitch (3). Take needle through point of emergence of first stitch (4/1). Bring needle out diagonally to the left (5), covering the same number of threads, and continue. You will now have a series of descending steps. To complete the squares, either return diagonally upwards to the right or turn the fabric and work exactly as before.

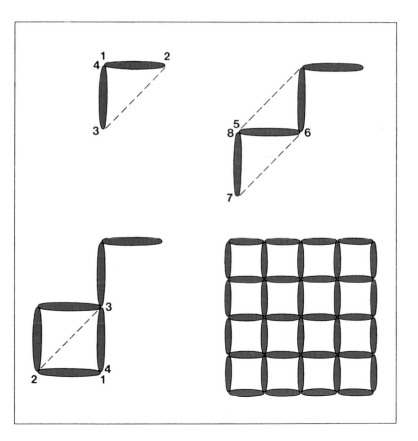

83

Swiss darning or Knitting stitch

This stitch looks like knitted stockinette stitch and is in fact frequently used to embroider knitting or to repair it. Swiss darning can also be used to cover large areas of canvas. As it is really a counted-thread stitch, the embroidery thread should be thick enough to cover the canvas or knitting underneath.

Swiss darning is worked vertically. Bring the thread through to right side of work and make a stitch to the left with the needle slanting diagonally upwards. As each new stitch is made, the thread should be brought through just below the previous one. This will make the left side of the stitches. To complete the right side, work upwards to the right of the stitches already made; it is important at this stage to ensure that the new row is made from the outside to the inside of the stitches, thus moving over to cover another vertical fabric thread, as shown in the illustration.

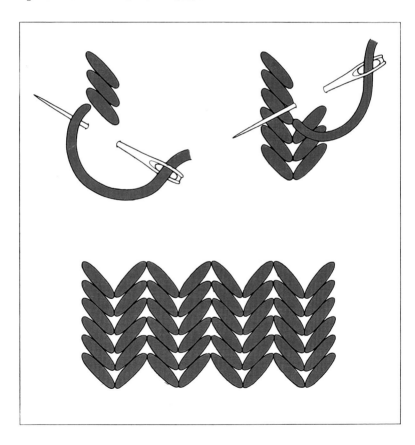

Overcast, Corded or Twisted bar

This stitch is also known as Sicilian drawn-thread stitch and is a method of embroidering on cut-and-drawn work or cut openwork. Best results can only be achieved on evenly woven fabrics of sufficient body not to fray. Stranded cotton (coton mouliné) is an ideal thread to use on most linen or linen-type fabrics but whatever is used should be of similar thickness to the threads of the fabric itself. This type of embroidery is mainly used on household linens, handkerchiefs and lingerie.

Start by withdrawing alternate groups of 4 threads from the fabric vertically and horizontally, following the instructions given (see page 53), to give a network effect. Now cover the remaining vertical bars with closely placed straight overcasting stitches (see page 41) and then work over the horizontal bars in the same way, thus forming small squares as illustrated. Complete the embroidery by overcasting all the outside edges of the design.

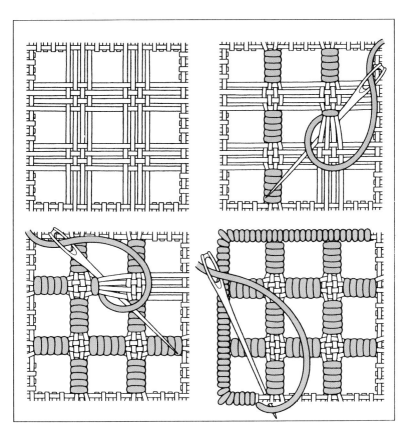

Overcast wheel stitch

This is rather a difficult stitch to do because the tension of the working thread has to be carefully maintained. It is advisable to practice on a spare piece of cloth before attempting to use the stitch definitively. The fabric to be embroidered should be very closely woven and the thread fine but strong.

Start by drawing a circle on the fabric about $\frac{1}{2}$–$\frac{3}{4}$ in (1–1.5 cm) in diameter and then, with small curved scissors, cut the central fabric away following the guide-line you have just drawn. Now embroider all round the cut edge in closely worked straight overcasting (see page 41).

The next step is to make the spokes, of which there can be from 6–12 depending on whether you want them close together or fairly widely spaced. However many you decide to have, they must be equidistant. Now attach the working thread neatly at the back of the overcast edging and make a loop towards the center of the wheel, bringing the needle back through the edging. Take the thread round the nearest side of the loop a few times until it covers about half its length and bring the needle back through the edging again, to the right of the first loop, to form another loop. Continue in the same way until you have made the required number of "spokes," each spoke consisting of half a loop. For the time being, half the first loop still remains uncovered.

To work the center circle or "hub", take the needle over and under the tops of all the linked loops, as shown in the picture. Now draw slightly on the working thread to get a firm, flat ring. Make sure the wheel is perfectly balanced.

Complete by taking the thread

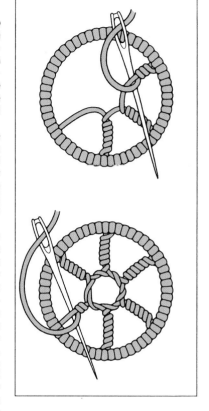

round the first spoke a few times and fasten off at the back of the overcast edging.

Guipure work

This is a style of cut-out embroidery which resembles heavy lace; its characteristic features are the independently worked bars bridging the spaces. All the edges of the design, as well as the bars, are worked in basic buttonhole stitch.

Although this style of work went

out of fashion some time ago, it has recently returned to favor with more stylized designs and colored fabrics, replacing the classic white on white.

As the fabric has to be cut away, it should have a certain amount of body to it; it is advisable to use pure cotton or a linen mixture. Stranded embroidery thread (coton mouliné) is recommended for this work.

Having transferred the design onto the fabric, it is helpful to baste the work to a piece of waxed paper (see page 24) with very long stitches. This will ensure that the fabric stays taut while you sew. Without putting the needle through the waxed paper, make an even row of running stitches (see page 39) over all the lines of the design to make a foundation for the button-hole stitching.

Working the bars first, bring the thread forward, back and forward again, picking up a small stitch on each side to anchor the 3 foundation threads. It is important to keep the tension of these threads exactly the same and they must not be too loose or too tight as the work would pucker. Take care not to pick up any of the fabric from underneath, during this stage. The needle will now be on the opposite side of the bar from the starting point. The next step is to cover the foundation threads with basic buttonholing (see page 42) until you return to the starting point.

Having completed all the bars, work over the rest of the design in basic buttonhole stitch. When the embroidery is finished, cut away the waxed paper.

Now using small curved scissors which should be very sharp, cut away all the excess fabric, taking great care to insert the scissors under the bars to avoid cutting them. The result will give a lacy effect.

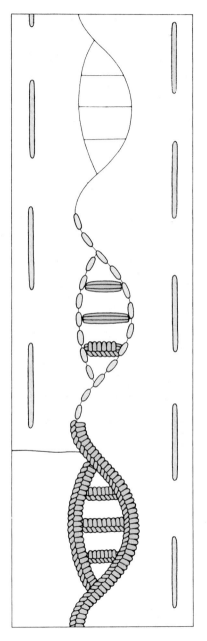

Richelieu work

This technique is the same as for Guipure work (see page 86) and is employed for the same purpose. The best threads to use are either linen, pearl cotton (coton perlé) or special stranded cotton (mouliné spécial).

For instructions as to how this is worked, please turn back to those given for Guipure work (page 86). The distinguishing features of Richelieu work are the tiny loops or "picots" which are worked on the bars, either singly or in twos. The type described here is known as a "bullion picot." To make one, put the needle through the last buttonhole stitch made on the foundation threads and wind the thread around it 7 or 8 times, as shown in top illustration. Pull the needle through, keeping the picot in place with the thumb and first finger of the left hand, and fasten picot down by inserting the needle back into the last buttonhole stitch.

The bar can now be completed by covering with buttonhole stitch but more picots can be worked, if required, at regular intervals.

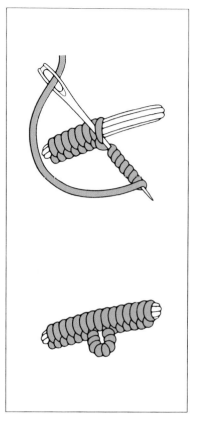

Renaissance work

This is a style of embroidery in which several types of stitch are employed. It is used both on borders and in the main body of bedspreads, tablecloths, etc., to produce an elegant, rich effect. The basic technique involves the use of a special type of braid, sold specifically for Renaissance work, and this is arranged into a design and kept in place by embroidered "bars" and by a kind of needlework mesh, both of which serve to embellish the work. The thread used should be fine but strong.

The first step is to draw or trace a design onto a piece of waxed paper (see page 24). Leaving $\frac{3}{4}$ in (2 cm) free, baste the braid (yellow in illustration) to the paper with running stitches. Where there are corners or tight curves, the braid will have to be folded before basting, in order for it to lie flat. At the beginning and at the end of the work leave $\frac{3}{4}$ in (2 cm) of braid free, fold over and secure under the edge of the fabric.

Now whipstitch (see page 41) all the edges of the braid, and work the embroidered bars as follows: being careful not to pick up the waxed paper with the needle, bring the thread across the space to be bridged and anchor it with a small stitch; repeat this in reverse and then return to the same point on the other side, maintaining the same tension with all three foundation threads. Cover this "bridge" in straight overcasting (see page 41) or in basic buttonhole stitch (see page 42).

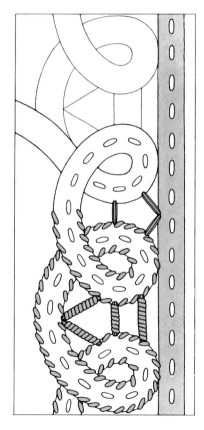

Smocking stitches

Smocking is a favorite method of embroidering children's clothes. It can be worked on any type of fabric that has a certain amount of body; very thin fabric is not suitable. A soft embroidery thread or pearl cotton (coton perlé) is best for the embroidery but a strong sewing cotton should be used for the gathering stitches.

Preparation of the fabric for smocking

Keeping the fabric taut and working on the wrong side from right to left, the first stage is to mark out a network of running stitches. The thread must be securely knotted at the beginning of each row and cut off at the end. The stitches should be about $\frac{5}{8}$ in (1.5 cm) apart on thicker fabrics and slightly closer on more delicate ones. The space between the rows can vary from about $\frac{3}{8}$ in (1 cm) upwards but must remain constant on each piece of work.

If the pattern has to converge towards a central point, such as a round neck, a paper pattern should be used. For this, a succession of concentric circles $\frac{3}{8}$ in (1 cm) apart can be drawn with a compass. Now draw an even number of dots $\frac{5}{8}$ in (1.5 cm) apart all round the smallest circle and mark up the other circles with the same number of dots, with the aid of a ruler. You will now have several rows of dots which all correspond to the first row but which get progressively farther apart as the circles widen. Now place the pattern on the fabric and apply one of the methods for tracing designs previously described (see pages 34–38), remembering that the gathering has

89

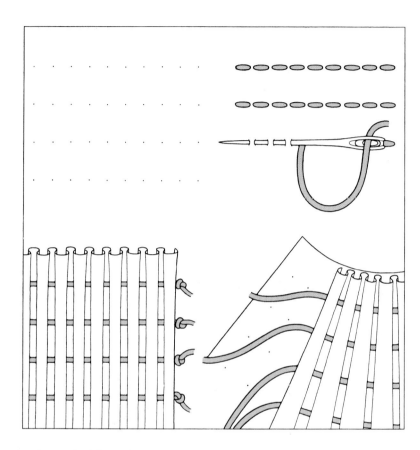

to be worked from the wrong side. Running stitches can now be worked from right to left, as already described, using the dots as markers for each stitch.

When all the rows have been worked, pull the free ends of thread and gather the fabric evenly until it reaches the desired measurement. You will now have a series of small pleats right across the fabric or round the yoke, if the gathers have been made in circles, in which case a center opening will have had to be made. Secure all the threads with a pin at the end of each row or fasten them off temporarily. When the embroidery has been worked, all the gathering threads can be withdrawn except the top and bottom ones which should be fastened off securely.

This completes the preparation and the decorative embroidery can now be worked on the right side of the fabric. The following are a few basic ideas for this but many other stitches can easily be adapted as decorative smocking stitches.

Trellis stitch smocking

This stitch is worked from left to right although the needle is inserted from right to left, starting from the first pleat on the left. Pull the thread through and work a backstitch (see page 40) over each of the next 4 pleats, keeping the thread below the needle. Each stitch should be 3 or 4 fabric threads above the previous one, to achieve the upward line. Work a single horizontal stitch over the fifth and sixth pleats and then repeat the process downwards.

Outline or stem stitch smocking

The same method is used as for basic stem stitch (see page 60), working from left to right with the needle pointing from right to left. Having picked up the first pleat and pulled the thread through, pick up the next one, keeping the thread under the needle which should point upwards, and pull the thread through. Continue in this way all along the row, maintaining an even tension throughout.

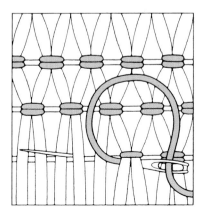

Honeycomb smocking stitch

Bringing the needle out through the center of the second pleat, keep the thread above it and insert it through the first and second pleats. Pull thread through and make a stitch, below the one just made, over the first pleat and bring needle through on the other side of the fourth pleat. Insert needle through the third and fourth pleats and repeat. Continue, alternating the pleats on the next row by working over the second and third, fourth and fifth, and so on.

91

Surface honeycomb smocking

Work from left to right on the lower row of gathering stitches. Join the first and second pleat with a horizontal stitch by bringing the needle out to the left of first pleat, insert it to the right of second and bring it out between the two pleats. Going to the upper row of gathering stitches, insert the needle through to the right of the second pleat and join the second and third pleats with a horizontal stitch. Return to the second row of gathering stitches and join the third and fourth pleats.

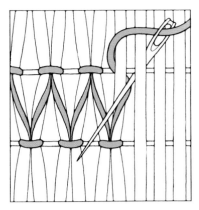

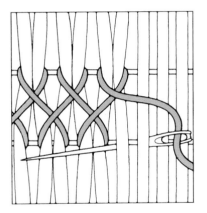

Cross stitch smocking

Working from left to right, start from the lower row of gathering stitches. Bring the needle through the center of the first pleat and, taking it up to the upper line of gathering stitches, insert it from right to left to join the second and first pleats. Return to the second row of gathering stitches and join the third and second pleats in the same way, by inserting the needle from right to left. Now go back to the first row and repeat the process. Continue to end of row.

Cross stitch

Basic cross stitch is certainly one of the easiest embroidery stitches but it is one with which some most striking effects can be achieved, especially in the subtle use of colors. All variations of cross stitch are based on symmetry and on a formalization of the design. Quite simple designs can often be worked directly on to the fabric by counting the threads and following a chart but more complicated ones are usually drawn on the fabric, sometimes with colored pencils that correspond to the colors shown for the embroidery. If the fabric is very fine or of an irregular weave, the design must be transferred on to it.

There are a great many variations of cross stitch and, although sometimes complicated, they are always most effective.

Vertical cross stitch

This is worked downwards, completing one stitch at a time. The needle is first inserted vertically to make a diagonal stitch to the right and then a diagonal stitch to the left to complete the cross, as shown in the illustration. This stitch can also be worked upwards in the same way, making the first stitch diagonally to the left and the second to the right.

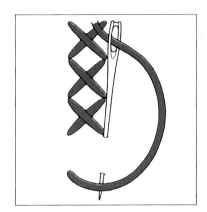

Horizontal cross stitch

This is worked in two stages, the first to the right and the second to the left. In the first stage, the needle is inserted into the fabric and brought out again vertically to form a row of diagonal stitches to the right; the second stage repeats the process, working from right to left, to produce diagonal stitches to the left which complete the crosses.

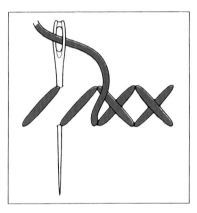

Double cross stitch

A row of horizontal cross stitches is worked first and then a row of horizontal stitches across the center of them. Finally, a row of perpendicular stitches is worked over the horizontal ones. The result is a series of perpendicular crosses over the diagonal ones.

93

Two-sided cross stitch

There are two different methods of working this stitch.

First method: this is worked in four stages, the first and third from right to left, the second and fourth from left to right. Having worked the first two stages, following the top diagram on the left, the result will be a zig-zag line. Then, still following the diagram, work the next two stages to complete the crosses. The effect will be the same on both sides of the work.

Second method: this is worked in two stages. The first forms the lower half of the diagonal stitch from right to left and the second from left to right. The diagram, below, shows the progress of the needle and thread to completion. With this method, too, the result is the same on both sides.

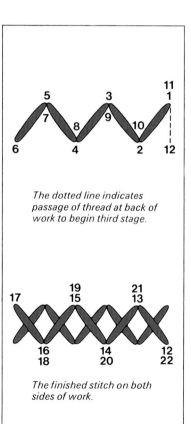

The dotted line indicates passage of thread at back of work to begin third stage.

The finished stitch on both sides of work.

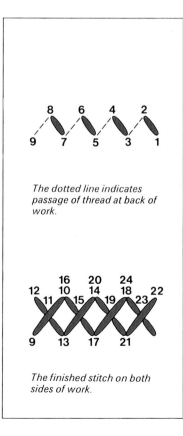

The dotted line indicates passage of thread at back of work.

The finished stitch on both sides of work.

Two-sided Italian cross stitch

There are four stages to this stitch, the first and third being worked from left to right and the second and fourth from right to left. The first stage is worked, as shown in the diagrams, from 1 to 15, repeating from 2 to 15 after the first stitch has been completed. In the second stage, the lower horizontal stitch is worked all along the row and in the third stage the upper horizontal stitches are worked on both sides of the fabric. The whole square is then completed in the fourth stage.

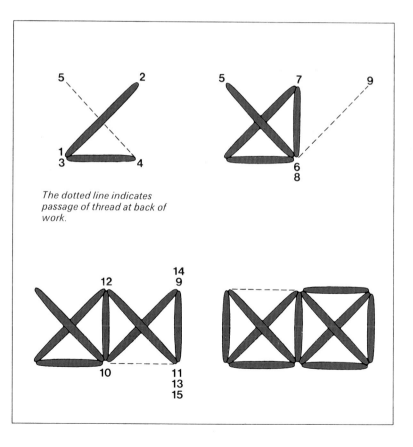

The dotted line indicates passage of thread at back of work.

Belgian cross stitch

This stitch is worked entirely in one stage, from left to right, following the diagram from 1 to 8. After completing the first stitch, repeat from 3 to 8.

Greek cross stitch

This stitch is worked entirely in one stage, from left to right, following the diagram from 1 to 9. After completing the first stitch, repeat from 4 to 9.

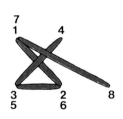

The dotted line indicates passage of thread at back of work.

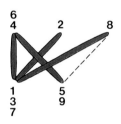

The dotted line indicates passage of thread at back of work.

The finished stitch.

The finished stitch.

Long-armed or Long-legged cross stitch

This stitch is worked entirely in one stage, from left to right, following the diagram from 1 to 7. After completing the first stitch, repeat from 4 to 7 to the end of the row.

The dotted line indicates passage of thread at back of work.

The finished stitch.

Russian cross stitch

This stitch is worked entirely in one stage, from left to right, following the diagrams from 1 to 15. After completing the first stitch, repeat from 12 to 15 to the end of the row. On the back of the work there will be a row of double parallel vertical stitches.

First part of stitch.

Horizontal extension of stitch.

Persian cross stitch

This stitch is worked entirely in one stage, from left to right, following the diagram from 1 to 6. After completing the first stitch, repeat from 3 to 6 to the end of the row.

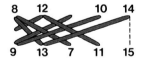

The finished stitch.

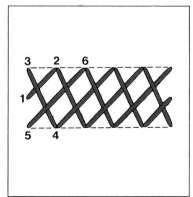

Armenian cross stitch or Double-threaded herringbone stitch

There are four stages to this stitch, the first and third being worked from left to right and the second and fourth from right to left. The various stages are clearly shown in the diagrams: the first pair demonstrates the two-stage basis of crossed stitches (herringbone over herringbone) and the second pair shows how the spirals are worked through them. An even tension is particularly important.

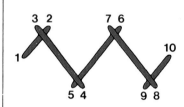

First stage of elongated cross (herringbone) stitch.

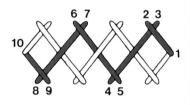

Second stage of elongated cross (herringbone) stitch.

Intertwining of first spiral.

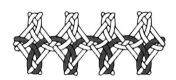

Intertwining of second spiral.

Double long-armed (or long-legged) cross stitch

This stitch is worked entirely in one stage, from left to right, following the top diagram from 1 to 9. After completing the first stitch, repeat from 6 to 9 to the end of the row. On the back of the work there will be vertical and diagonal stitches alternately.

Diagonal cross stitch

Working upwards, make the first diagonal stitch from left to right and the second from right to left, bringing the needle out at the point where the next stitch is to start (top diagram).

This stitch can also be worked downwards in a single stage. Working from right to left, make a diagonal stitch to the left and complete the cross with another diagonal stitch to the right (bottom diagram).

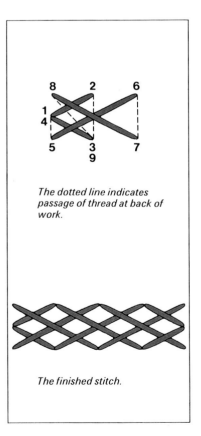

The dotted line indicates passage of thread at back of work.

The finished stitch.

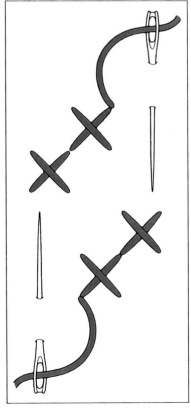

Assisi work

This is a style of counted-thread embroidery and it is therefore essential to use an evenly woven fabric, the ideal, of course, being Assisi linen. Any type of embroidery thread can be used, providing it is in proportion to the fabric. The background of Assisi work is always in cross stitch while the design, which is left plain, is outlined in Holbein (double running) stitch. The subject of the design is usually based on geometric motifs or animals.

The outlines should be worked first in Holbein (double running) stitch; this is similar to running stitch (see page 39) in which an equal number of threads is picked up and passed over, working from right to left. By turning the work, the spaces are covered with another group of running stitches. The background can then be filled in by working vertical and horizontal cross stitch (see page 93). Any designs around the edge can be completed in Holbein stitch or backstitch (see page 40).

Gobelin stitches

These stitches are usually used to cover large areas when making canvas work, or needlepoint, pictures, wall hangings, etc. They can be worked on single or double mesh canvas, using tapestry yarn, stranded cotton (coton mouliné) or soft embroidery cotton. The thread must always be in proportion to the canvas and a tapestry needle (these have a blunt end) of the right size to take the thread comfortably should be used.

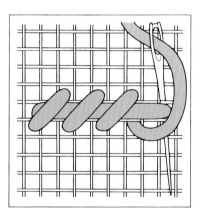

Half Gobelin stitch

Having worked a long padding stitch (see page 39) from right to left, bring the needle out through the space directly below the end of it. Passing over two vertical threads to the right and over the padding stitch, insert the needle and bring it through again in the second space immediately underneath. The stitches will be vertically parallel on the wrong side.

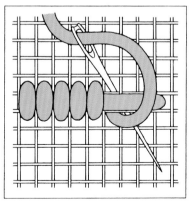

Straight or Upright Gobelin stitch

This is worked in the same way as the half Gobelin except that the needle is taken diagonally downwards, leaving only one thread between the stitches. Remember always to start with a long padding stitch (see page 39). The stitches will be diagonally parallel on the wrong side.

Oblique Gobelin stitch

This is worked in the same way as
the half Gobelin over 1 vertical and 2
horizontal   threads.   Remember
always to start with a long padding
stitch (see page 39). The stitches
will be vertically parallel and close
together on the wrong side.

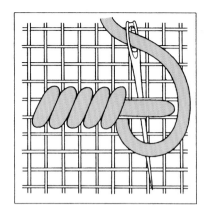

Tent stitch or Gros point (in soft
embroidery cotton or tapestry yarn)

Petit point (in silk or 3 strands of
stranded cotton on fine canvas)

This can be worked in two ways:
1. The rows are worked back and
forth starting from the right with an
upward diagonal stitch to the right
but with the needle carried down to
the left. The thread is then carried
under 2 of the canvas threads on the
wrong side, as shown at the top of
the illustration on the left. On the
return row, the needle is carried
diagonally up to the right.
2. The rows are only worked in one
direction, starting with a long padding stitch (see page 39) on the
back (or front) from left to right.
Cover this with oblique Gobelin
stitches to the right and on the row
beneath, work a small stitch. Now
make another long padding stitch
from left to right and cover it, from
right to left, in the same way, as
shown in the illustration below right.
The stitches on the wrong side will
be diagonal and rather long.

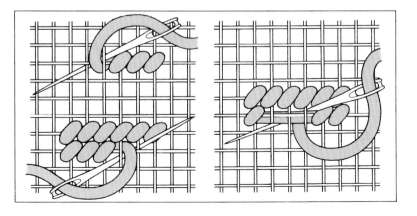

Woven stitch

Woven stitch is worked on wide-meshed single or double thread canvas with tapestry yarn, soft embroidery cotton or special stranded cotton (mouliné spécial), depending on the weight of canvas being used. It is an easy stitch and particularly suitable for large areas of groundwork or for embroidering geometric and stylized figures.

Work in the same way as running stitches (see page 39), over counted threads, either vertically, horizontally or diagonally, according to the design. The illustration shows an example of woven stitch worked horizontally.

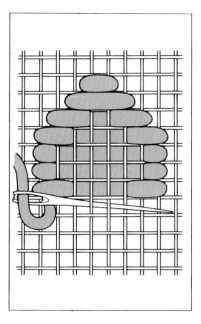

Byzantine stitch

This stitch is worked on single or double thread canvas with soft embroidery cotton, tapestry yarn, wool or special stranded cotton (mouliné spécial), depending on the weight of canvas being used. It is an easy stitch and particularly suitable for covering large areas of background.

Working diagonally over 2 canvas threads, make 5 stitches in a vertical direction and 5 in a horizontal direction. Continue as desired, alternating the groups of stitches in the same way. Spaces left unworked are filled up with a few similar stitches and even an occasional tent stitch.

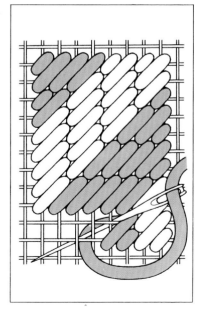

Checkerboard stitch

This stitch is worked on single or double thread canvas with tapestry yarn, special stranded cotton (mouliné spécial) or soft embroidery cotton. It is useful for large areas of groundwork and can be worked in alternating colors.

Working back and forth from left to right and then from right to left, make 5 vertical stitches over 4 canvas threads followed by 5 horizontal stitches over 4 canvas threads. Complete the row in the same way. On the return row, work 5 horizontal stitches under the vertical ones of the previous row and 5 vertical stitches under the horizontal ones.

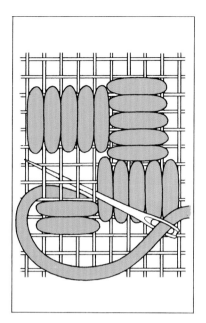

Florentine or Flame stitch

This stitch can be worked on single or double thread canvas. Its effectiveness is achieved by the changes of color worked into the undulating designs formed by this stitch. There is no fixed number of canvas threads over which to work as this will depend upon the effect you wish to achieve. The canvas must be completely covered by the embroidery and the thread used may be tapestry yarn, special stranded cotton (mouliné spécial) or soft embroidery cotton, depending upon the weight of canvas.

Always working vertically, each stitch may cover 2 or more canvas threads. The illustration shows the beginning of a design worked in Florentine (Flame) stitch.

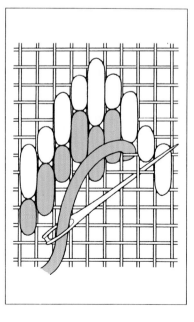

Linen stitch

This stitch is worked on single or double thread canvas with soft embroidery cotton, tapestry yarn or special stranded cotton (mouliné spécial). It is an effective and unusual way of covering large background areas or of filling in spaces.

Traveling diagonally from left to right, the first row is worked downwards, covering 2 canvas threads horizontally, and moving the stitch 1 canvas thread to the left each time. The second row is worked upwards, covering 2 canvas threads vertically, and moving the stitch one canvas thread upwards each time, as shown in the illustration.

Rhodes canvas stitch

This stitch can only be worked on single thread canvas in tapestry yarn, soft embroidery cotton or special stranded cotton (mouliné spécial). It may be used for groundwork for filling in or even for decorative motifs.

Rhodes canvas stitch is always worked on a square section of the canvas over any number of threads. The illustration shows quite clearly the journeys made by the embroidery thread, up to completion of the square. To finish off the center, work a small vertical stitch to cover all the threads and take the needle to the back through the canvas. Finish off neatly on the wrong side.

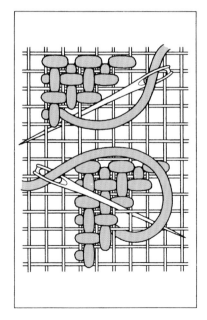

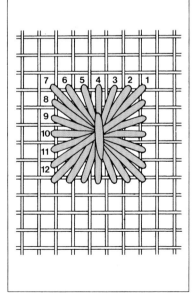

Carpet or rug stitches

For rug making, the two most
suitable stitches are Velvet stitch and
Smyrna (single knotted) stitch. The
result is reminiscent of oriental car-
pets and such rugs are usually made
with a specially twisted thick wool
on a large-mesh, single or double
thread canvas. The stitches must be
completely regular and this is
achieved by using a small piece of
wood to control the size of the
stitches.

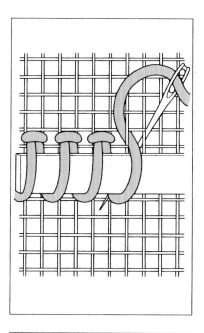

Velvet rug stitch

Working downwards from left to
right, follow the diagram closely,
making sure that the wool is not
pulled tightly round the wooden
gauge.

Smyrna (single knotted) rug stitch

This is worked in the same way as
Velvet rug stitch except that the
loops round the wooden gauge must
be cut and trimmed to the desired
length at the end of each row, being
very careful not to cut them too
short.

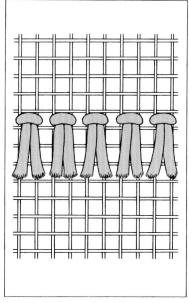

Stitches for appliqué work

Appliqué work, which is merely the stitching of one piece of cloth on to almost any kind of fabric foundation, can be done in various ways. Suitable stitches are: straight overcasting (see page 41), basic buttonhole stitch (see page 42), Paris stitch (see page 45), stem stitch (see page 60) and many others. The preparation of the pieces is always the same: first of all, having checked that the grain of both fabrics is going the same way, draw the outlines of the shapes on the fabric to be applied and cut them out, leaving a margin of about $\frac{3}{16}$ in (5 mm) all around. Now baste (see page 40) the cut-out shape onto the foundation, making sure that it is in exactly the correct position, the stitches being about $\frac{3}{16}$ in (5 mm) from the edge.

The preparation is now complete and the application itself can be undertaken. Having decided which stitch to use, turn the edge under gradually as you work round it. Sometimes the fabric being applied may have very irregular or frayed edges and it will not be possible to turn them in; in this case, using a very closely worked stitch, such as basic buttonholing (see page 42), sew the cut-out shape onto the foundation fabric and cut away the excess fabric, taking great care not to cut the stitches.

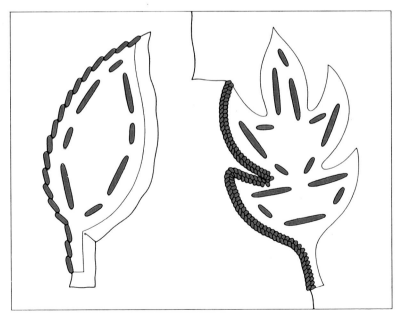

New and traditional ideas: 53 practical suggestions

The following projects show how you can use the stitches described earlier in this book. In most cases, the exact gauge of canvas used in the needlework projects has been left up to you as you will want to utilize the designs given here for your own purposes. Just be sure to count the stitches on the charts shown here, to center your designs and work out the proportions of canvas. Use embroidery or needlepoint thread suitable to the canvas you have chosen.

Embroidery designs which are shown worked on sweaters, nightgowns or bathrobes here can just as easily be transferred to knitted hats, mittens, scarves or many other projects as is true of all the designs. You are limited only by your imagination.

When using the designs on grids here be sure to enlarge them to the proportions you need by following the instructions given at the beginning of this book.

HOT-WATER BOTTLE COVER

Materials: a piece of blue cotton fabric; pearl cotton (coton perlé) in light green, dark green, red, yellow, dark blue, orange, pink, black and mauve; $1\frac{2}{3}$ yd (1.5 m) of 2 in (5 cm) wide bias binding in a blue and white design; a few snap fasteners.

Stitches: basic stem stitch (see page 60), French knot (see page 80), padded satin stitch (see page 76) and backstitch (see page 40).

Measurements: see bottom diagram.

Making the cover: cut two identical pieces from the fabric, on the straight grain (see page 53), taking the measurements from the diagram. With right sides of fabric facing, sew the two pieces together but leave the rounded part at the bottom free. Turn the right side outwards and transfer the design onto one side.

Using the same colors as in the photograph, work the petals, stalks, leaves and wings of the butterfly in basic stem stitch, the flower centers in French knots and the markings on the butterfly in padded satin stitch. Fold the bias binding in half lengthwise and, having pinned and basted it carefully over both lower edges, backstitch neatly into position, making sure the stitches go through to the wrong side. Sew snap fasteners about $1\frac{1}{2}$ in (4 cm) apart along inside edges. Press cover under a damp cloth, using a fairly hot iron.

$5\frac{3}{4}$ in = 15 cm
$8\frac{1}{4}$ in = 21 cm
11 in = 28 cm
$17\frac{1}{2}$ in = 45 cm

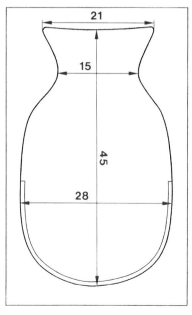

21

15

45

28

TABLE NAPKINS AND PLACEMATS

Materials: beige cotton fabric; 2 balls of pearl cotton (coton perlé) in red and green; strong sewing thread (beige).

Stitches: chain stitch (see page 61) and hemstitch (see page 45).

Measurements: placemats measure 24×16 in (60×40 cm) and the napkins 12×12 in (30×30 cm), including $\frac{3}{4}$ in (2 cm) for the fringe.

Making the napkins and placemats: cut out the napkins and placemats on the straight grain (see page 53), using the measurements above. Transfer the design to each corner of the placemats, about $2\frac{3}{4}$ in (7 cm) from the edge. On the napkins, the design is only repeated twice, on the diagonally opposing corners.

Work all the motifs in chain stitch, taking care to maintain a fairly easy tension so that the fabric lies flat.

To make the fringe, withdraw 2 fabric threads (see page 53) $\frac{3}{4}$ in (2 cm) from the outside edge. Working on the wrong side, hemstitch all the way round, securing the threads in groups of 5 or 6 and taking the working thread over towards the embroidered area. Complete the fringe by withdrawing the rest of the fabric threads from all the sides.

Press the placemats and napkins on the wrong side, under a damp cloth, with a fairly hot iron; do not press too heavily, however, to avoid flattening the embroidery.

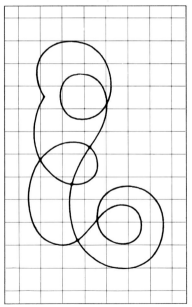

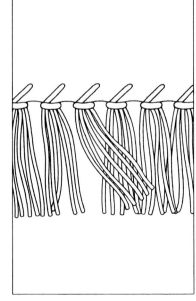

TEA-TOWEL, POT HOLDER AND OVEN GLOVE

Materials: white cotton fabric, such as pique; about $4\frac{1}{2}$ yd (4 m) of yellow cotton binding or ribbon; 1 ball of blue pearl cotton (coton perlé); a little yellow pearl cotton; some thick, heat-resistant fabric for padding.

Stitches: basic feather stitch (see page 63) and backstitch (page 40).

Measurements: tea-towel $27\frac{1}{2} \times 27\frac{1}{2}$ in $(70 \times 70$ cm), pot holder $6\frac{3}{4} \times 6\frac{3}{4}$ in $(17 \times 17$ cm). For glove measurements see diagram.

Making the tea-towel: using the measurements indicated above, cut out the tea-towel, on the straight grain (see page 53).
　　Fold the binding in half lengthwise, pin and baste it all around the edges, and secure it with closely worked backstitch, making sure that the stitches go through to the wrong side. With the blue pearl cotton, work a row of basic feather stitch along all four sides, $\frac{3}{4}$ in (2 cm) from the yellow border. Make a loop (see page 57) at one corner, using the blue and yellow cottons.

Making the pot holder: cut out a piece of fabric on the straight grain (see page 53), using the measurements indicated above, and also a piece of the thick material. Join the pieces together by working in backstitch all the way around. Bind the holder with binding. On the plain cotton side (right side) of the holder, work a row of basic feather stitch in blue pearl cotton along each side,

$\frac{1}{2}$ in (1 cm) from the yellow border. Make a loop at one corner.

Making the glove: fold fabric in half, right sides together, and cut out the glove shape and two pieces of the thick fabric. (See diagram.)
　　Sew one of the thick fabric shapes to the wrong side of each of the plain cotton shapes and then join them all together, right sides inwards, with closely worked backstitch, leaving the wrist open. Turn glove right side outwards and bind wrist opening with the yellow binding. Work a row of blue feather stitch around the wrist, $\frac{1}{2}$ in (1 cm) from the yellow border. Make a loop.

$1\frac{1}{2}$ in = 3.5 cm
4 in = 10.5 cm
$4\frac{3}{4}$ in = 12.5 cm
$6\frac{1}{4}$ in = 16 cm
$11\frac{3}{4}$ in = 30 cm

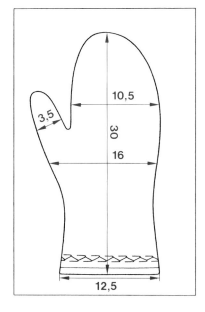

SMALL TABLECLOTH IN LAZY DAISY STITCH

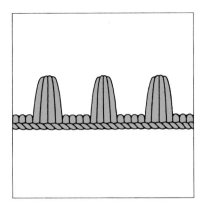

Materials: white linen (for measurements, see below); 3 balls of each of the following colors in pearl cotton (coton perlé): green, yellow, pink, light blue, mauve, brown, dark blue.

Stitches: lazy daisy stitch (see page 65), French knot (see page 80), encroaching stem stitch (see page 60) and buttonhole stitch (see page 42).

Measurements: 40 × 30 in (1 m × 75 cm) plus ¾ in (2 cm) for the hem.

Making the cloth: cut the linen to the required size, on the straight grain (see page 53). Transfer the design

onto each side 3 in (8 cm) from the outside edge and the circlet of flowers in the center (10 in [25 cm]) from the edge. Work the petals and leaves in lazy daisy stitch, the stems in encroaching stem stitch and the centers in French knots. Make a ¾-in (2-cm) hem (see pages 54–55) and decorate the edges with long and short buttonhole stitch, as above.

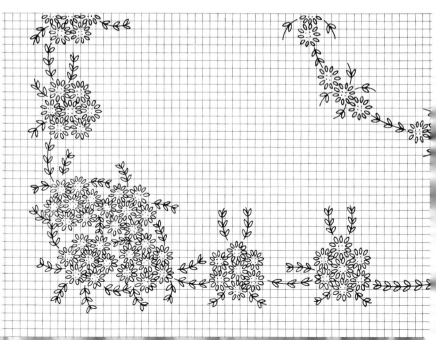

CUSHION COVER IN CORAL STITCH

Materials: turquoise silk (see below for measurements); 2 skeins of stranded embroidery cotton; 12 in (30 cm) zipper; pillow form or cotton batting.

Stitches: coral stitch (see page 67) and backstitch (see page 40).

Measurements: 16 × 16 in (40 × 40 cm) plus $\frac{3}{4}$ in (2 cm) for the seams.

Making the cover: cut two squares of silk to the measurements given above. Place the two pieces together, right sides facing, and join them on three sides using close backstitch. On the fourth side, sew up only $1\frac{1}{2}$ in (4 cm) at each end. Turn right side out and draw or transfer the motif on one side of the cover. Work the whole design in coral stitch, paying particular attention to the regularity of the lines and to maintaining an even tension. Now sew the zipper into the opening on the fourth side, using close backstitch.

Press the cushion cover lightly on the wrong side with a cool iron. Insert the pillow form which should be exactly the same size as the cover, or stuff with cotton batting and close the zipper.

ROUND TRAYCLOTH AND COASTERS

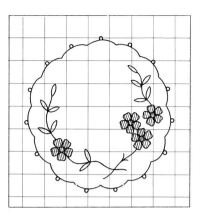

Materials: some fine linen in ivory; 2 balls of pearl cotton (coton perlé) in each of the following colors: yellow ochre, yellow, 2 shades of green and 3 shades of light blue.

Stitches: Bokhara couching (see page 68), stem stitch (see page 60), padded satin stitch (see page 76) and buttonhole stitch (see page 42).

Measurements: the traycloth is 16 in (40 cm) in diameter and the coasters 5½ in (14 cm). Allow a border of ¾ in (2 cm) all around, which will ultimately be cut off.

Making the traycloth and coasters: cut out a circle for the traycloth and 6 smaller ones for the coasters, following the measurements given above. Transfer the designs from the diagrams, making sure they are properly centered, and work the flowers, leaves and stems in Bokhara couching, stem stitch and padded satin stitch, alternating the stitches and colors as shown in the photograph. Now transfer the scalloped edging following the proportions indicated in the diagrams, on to the traycloth and coasters, keeping it ¾ in (2 cm) away from the edge. Work over the scallops in buttonhole stitch, keeping the firm edge facing away from the embroidery. Cut the excess fabric away with sharp, curved scissors, taking great care not to spoil the buttonhole stitching. Finally work picot, as described in the instructions for Richelieu work (see page 88), at the top of each scallop.

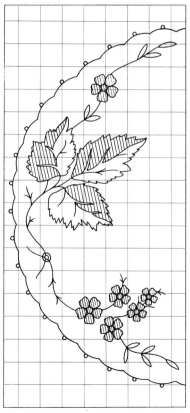

DECORATIVE TABLE MAT

Materials: a piece of white cotton fabric; 3 skeins of stranded embroidery cotton in each of the following colors: green, yellow and 2 shades of pink and brown.

Stitches: padded satin stitch (see page 76), stem stitch (see page 60), buttonhole scalloping (see page 69).

Measurements: 24 × 16 in (61 × 40 cm). Allow a border of ¾ in (2 cm) all around, which will ultimately be cut off.

Making the mat: cut the mat out,

using the measurements given above, and transfer the design onto it, making sure it is properly centered. Work all the central motifs first, using padded satin stitch for the flowers, leaves and ribbons, and stem stitch for the stems. The colored photograph will serve as a guide to the use of the colors.

The scalloped edging can now be drawn in, following the diagram, leaving at least ¾ in (2 cm) of fabric all around the edge. Work the scallops and scrolls with yellow thread, in buttonhole scalloping. Carefully cut away the excess fabric with small, sharp curved scissors. Spray a little starch over the mat and, on the wrong side, press lightly over a thick pad with a moderately hot iron so that the embroidery will be slightly raised.

TABLECLOTH AND TABLE NAPKINS IN SATIN STITCH

Materials: white cotton fabric (see below for measurements); 3 skeins of stranded embroidery cotton in each of the following colors: white, pink, 2 shades of red, 2 shades of green, light blue and beige.

Stitches: satin stitch (see page 71), stem stitch (see page 60), padded satin stitch (see page 76), broderie anglaise (see page 72), buttonhole stitch (see page 42).

Measurements: the tablecloth measures 33 × 33 in (84 × 84 cm) and the napkins 10 × 10 in (25 × 25 cm). Allow extra ¾ in (2 cm) on all the sides; this will be cut off after the edging has been worked.

Making the cloth and napkins: cut out the cloth and napkins, on the straight grain (see page 53), according to the measurements given above. Transfer the design onto the cloth and the small spray onto one corner of each napkin. Work the buds, roses and leaves in satin stitch, the blue stars and pink crosses in padded satin stitch, the small holes in broderie anglaise and the blue flowers and all the other motifs in stem stitch. Work in buttonhole stitch all around the cloth and napkins, ¾ in (2 cm) from the edge.

Complete the work by cutting away the excess fabric and pressing carefully, on the wrong side, using a damp cloth.

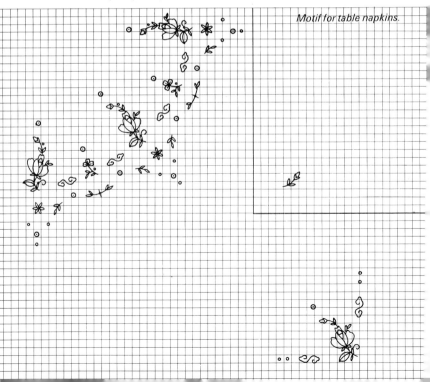

Motif for table napkins.

BUDS AND A BUTTERFLY FOR A CARDIGAN

Materials: small amounts of 2-ply wool in the following colors: white, 3 shades of pink, 2 shades of yellow, mauve, violet and beige.

Stitches: satin stitch (see page 71), padded satin stitch (see page 76), stem stitch (see page 60).

Measurements: the embroidery, as shown in illustration, measures approximately $7 \times 5\frac{1}{2}$ in $(18 \times 14$ cm) and the cardigan is a ladies' size.

Embroidery on knitting: although the design, as illustrated, has been worked on a handknitted cardigan, the same embroidery could be worked on a machine knitted garment to give it individuality or even on an old one to brighten it up. It could also be worked on the front or on pockets instead of the shoulder.

Trace the design onto tissue paper and baste in place on the cardigan. Working through the tissue, work the wings and antennae of the butterfly in stem stitch, the body of the butterfly, stems and leaves in padded satin stitch and the flowers in basic satin stitch. When working in wool on wool, it is essential to keep the tension of the stitches even and fairly loose, to give elasticity. Tear away the tissue when finished.

The embroidery should not be pressed as it would be inclined to flatten and lose its three-dimensional appearance.

SATIN STITCH EMBROIDERED HAND-TOWELS

Materials: reversible beige linen; 1 skein of embroidery silk in each of the following colors: for one towel, shaded yellow, shaded green, chestnut brown, rusty brown; for the other towel, shaded pale green, shaded pink, shaded yellow, chestnut brown and a rich red; linen (or strong cotton) thread in beige.

Stitches: Chinese (Jacobean) satin stitch (see page 72), long and short satin stitch (see page 71), padded satin stitch (see page 76), stem stitch (see page 60), French knots (see page 80) and hemstitching with isolated overcast bars (see page 48).

Measurements: each hand-towel measures about 25×16 in (64×41 cm) plus $\frac{3}{4}$ in (2 cm) on each short side and $\frac{1}{4}$ in (0.5 cm) on each long side for the hems. The embroidery measures about $8\frac{1}{2} \times 3$ in (22×8 cm).

Making the towels: following the measurements given above, cut out the linen exactly on the straight grain (see page 53). Fold the long sides over $\frac{1}{4}$ in (0.5 cm) and hem neatly in place (see pages 54–55) with the matching thread. Withdraw 4 fabric threads (see page 53) about $\frac{3}{4}$ in (2 cm) from the edges of the short sides and hemstitch with isolated overcast bars, using the matching thread. Transfer the design onto one side of each towel $1\frac{1}{2}$ in (4 cm) from the hemstitching at one end, making

sure it is perfectly centered. Work the petals in Chinese (Jacobean) satin stitch, changing color as shown in the photograph. The leaves can then be worked in long and short satin stitch, the buds in padded satin stitch and the center of the large flower in French knots. The stems and veins of the leaves are worked in ordinary stem stitch.

Press the embroidery on the wrong side, using a damp cloth and a well padded ironing board.

CHINESE SHAWL IN SATIN STITCH

Materials: a length of dark brown or black silk; 15 skeins of embroidery silk in each of the following colors: 5 shades of green, 4 shades of light blue, 4 shades of pink, 2 shades of violet, 2 shades of yellow ochre and 2 shades of yellow; 50 skeins of dark brown or black embroidery silk the same shade as the fabric.

Stitches: Chinese (Jacobean) satin stitch (see page 72), long and short satin stitch (see page 71), stem stitch (see page 60), basting (see page 40).

Measurements: the shawl measures about 70 × 70 in (175 × 175 cm) plus $\frac{3}{4}$ in (2 cm) all around for the hems. The fringe measures 12 in (30 cm) but is added after the embroidery has been worked.

Making the shawl: first of all, the fabric must be prepared with great accuracy. Silk is very delicate and must, therefore, be handled with great care, especially in the cutting. Cut out a square on the straight grain of the fabric (see page 53), according to the measurements given above.

A hem can now be worked along all four edges; this should be folded over three times, taking up $\frac{3}{4}$ in (2 cm) allowance all around, basted and then hemmed as described on pages 54–55. When the hems have been completed, the design, which is given on pages 132–133, can be transferred onto all four corners about 2 in (5 cm) from the edges. In doing this, care must be taken to work out the measurements and

proportions accurately so that each design is centered exactly in the four corners. As the great charm of this type of work is its detail, all the delineations shown on the inside of the outlines to indicate color shadings must be marked on the transferred design.

All the motifs in which color shadings are indicated in the design will, therefore, be worked in Chinese (Jacobean) satin stitch; all the others, flowers, leaves, branches and so on, should be worked in ordinary satin stitch, sometimes in one color only. The only exceptions are the slender stems which are better worked in ordinary stem stitch.

The changes of color and stitches, combined with the fine embroidery silk and delicate fabric, do not make this an easy piece of work to do. The tension of the working thread is particularly important; it must be kept perfectly even and slightly elastic throughout as any tendency to pucker would destroy the beauty of the work. As the embroidery proceeds, remember to refer constantly not only to the drawing of the design itself and the enlarged detail but also to the color photograph of a complete corner and to the color detail (see page 135) for guidance as to color changes, control of shading, etc.

To make the fringe, cut the dark brown or black silk thread into lengths of 32 in (80 cm). Divide into groups of three and fold in half. Using a needle which is as fine as possible but which has a large enough eye to take all three strands, make a small stitch on the wrong side of work, pull it into a loop and bring all the strands through the loop to the front, as shown in diagram. Repeat this at intervals of $\frac{3}{16}$ in (1 cm) along all four sides. Now they can be

Left, design of a quarter of the shawl described on the previous page; above, enlarged detail.

knotted, as shown, taking 3 strands from each group and knotting them in alternate rows until a network of about 4 in (10 cm) has been made. The rest of the silk threads are left to hang loose to form the actual fringe.

The work can now be carefully pressed, with a cool iron and a dry cloth over a well padded board. It is very important not to press too hard or the embroidery will be flattened.

The shawl which has been de-scribed here is an original example from the nineteenth century. The pattern and colors, which are inspired by Chinese art, show up particularly well against the dark background of the silk to create a truly sumptuous appearance and yet, at the same time, it has a delicate charm. It is certainly most elegant and will always be greatly admired, more than repaying all the hard work and care that has been put into it.

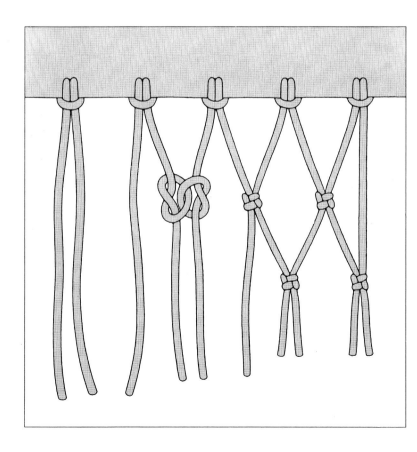

HANDKERCHIEF SACHET

Materials: a piece of white cotton organdy; 2 skeins of embroidery silk in each of the following colors: sky blue, dark blue, green, 2 shades of mauve and 3 shades of red, pink and yellow; 24 in (60 cm) of blue ribbon.

Stitches: Chinese (Jacobean) satin stitch (see page 72), separate Algerian eye stitch (see page 81), stem stitch (see page 60), straight stitch (see page 73), buttonhole stitch (see page 42).

Measurements: the whole strip of fabric that will go to making up the handkerchief sachet should measure $16\frac{1}{2} \times 7\frac{1}{2}$ in (42×19 cm) and allowance must be made for a $\frac{3}{4}$ in (2 cm) border which will later be cut away.

Making the handkerchief sachet: work in buttonhole stitch along all four sides about $\frac{3}{4}$ in (2 cm) from the outside edges. Now cut away the excess fabric with small sharp, curved scissors. Fold the fabric in half and work another row of but-

tonholing down the middle, as shown in the diagram. Transfer the design into the left-hand square and work as follows: the frame in stem stitch, the stars in Algerian eye stitch, the tulips and campanulas in satin stitch, the stems in stem stitch and the tulip leaves in straight stitches, changing color as shown.

As organdy is a particularly delicate fabric, it is essential for an even tension to be maintained.

Complete the sachet by cutting the ribbon in half and sewing one end at the center of each of the shorter sides. To close the sachet, tie the ribbons together loosely.

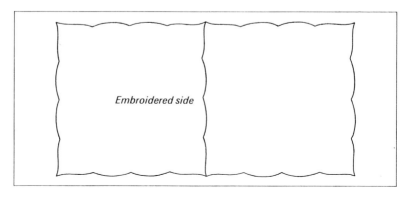

Embroidered side

NIGHTGOWN IN BRODERIE ANGLAISE

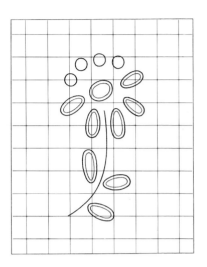

Materials: embroidery cotton, special quality (coton à broder, qualité spéciale) No. 60 in pink.

Stitches: broderie anglaise (see page 72) and stem stitch (see page 60).

Measurements: each flower measures about $1\frac{1}{2} \times \frac{3}{4}$ in (4 × 2 cm) and the nightgown shown here is a ladies' size.

Working the flowers: this very simple floral motif is worked on the front of a pink satin nightgown. First of all, transfer the flower motif several times onto the top front of the garment, arranged as shown in the illustration. Now, using the pink embroidery cotton, work the flowers in broderie anglaise and the stems in stem stitch. When the embroidery is complete, cut away the fabric from the center of the flowers, petals and leaves using small, curved scissors and being very careful not to ruin the embroidery by cutting the stitches.

Press the work on the wrong side over a well padded ironing board and under a damp cloth. The iron should be cool and great care should be taken to ensure that the embroidery stands out well.

The same floral motif, when embroidered with a similar technique, may also be used on baby clothes, vests, bibs, household linen, blouses and any other garments that can be improved by the addition of dainty embroidery that enhances the fabric.

TOP SHEET IN BRODERIE ANGLAISE

Materials: white linen; 5 skeins of stranded embroidery cotton in white; strong white sewing thread.

Stitches: broderie anglaise (see page 72), ladder hemstitch (see page 46), openwork strip with one row of clusters (see page 51) and shadow stitch (see page 79).

Measurements: a double sheet will require a piece of sheeting 104 × 87 in (264 × 220 cm) plus 2½ in (6 cm) all around for the hems.

Making the sheet: cut the fabric on the straight grain (see page 53), and withdraw 4 fabric threads (see page 53) 2½ in (6 cm) from the edge on all four sides. Fold the hem in half and work all the way around in ladder hemstitch and complete each corner as explained on page 52.

Transfer the motifs to the sheet, placing one in each corner and another in the center. Withdraw 20 fabric threads 4¾ in (12 cm) from the hemstitching for 32 in (80 cm) on each of the longer sides and, on the short side, between the motifs, (see diagram and photograph). Work the openwork strips.

With the white embroidery thread work the motifs as follows: the flowers in broderie anglaise and the ribbon bows in shadow stitch, working on the right side, so that the crossed stitches are uppermost. Cut away the openwork areas with very sharp, curved scissors.

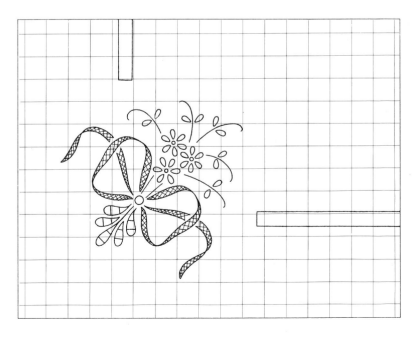

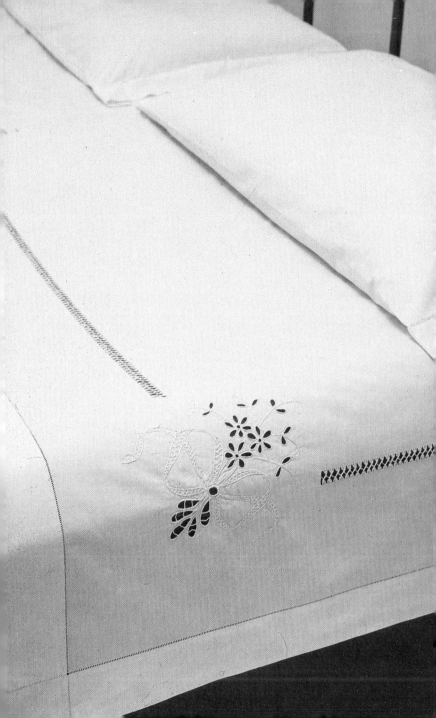

TABLE CENTER IN BRODERIE ANGLAISE

Materials: cotton embroidery fabric in white; 2 skeins of white stranded embroidery cotton; strong white sewing thread.

Stitches: ladder hemstitch (see page 46), broderie anglaise (see page 72), serpentine (trellis) hem-stitch (see page 46).

Measurements: 14×14 in (36×36 cm) plus 1 in (4 cm) for the hems.

Making the table center: having cut the fabric to the above measurements and making sure it is on the straight grain (see page 53), withdraw 3 fabric threads (see page 53) about $1\frac{1}{2}$ in (4 cm) from the edge on all four sides. Fold the hem in half and work all the way around in ladder hemstitch, using the strong thread. Transfer the motifs onto the fabric and work them in broderie anglaise, using the embroidery thread. Cut away the open-work areas with very sharp, curved scissors.

Withdraw 6 fabric threads at a distance of $1\frac{1}{4}$ in (3 cm) from the ladder hem-stitching, between the corner motifs, and work in serpentine (trellis) hem-stitch, using the strong thread.

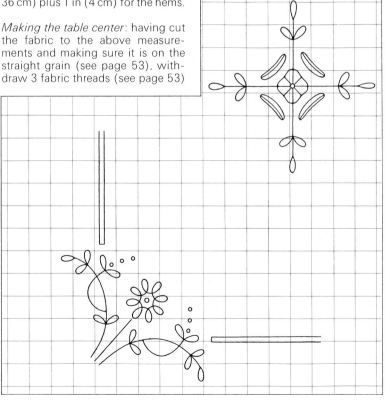

SMALL TABLECLOTH AND NAPKINS

Materials: cotton embroidery fabric in pale pink; 6 skeins of pearl cotton (coton perlé) in sky blue; strong white sewing thread.

Stitches: Palestrina (double knot) stitch (see page 74), padded satin stitch (see page 76), stem stitch (see page 60), simple hem-stitch (see page 45).

Measurements: the cloth measures 34×30 in (86×76 cm) and the napkins 7×7 in (18×18 cm). Allow $\frac{3}{4}$ in (2 cm) all around cloth and napkins for hem.

Making the cloth and napkins: having cut out the cloth and napkins, on the straight grain (see page 53), withdraw 3 fabric threads (see page 53) $\frac{3}{4}$ in (2 cm) from the edge on all four sides of each item. Fold the hems in half and work in simple hemstitch.

Now transfer the whole design onto the cloth. Using the pearl cotton, work the leafy line in Palestrina (double knot) stitch, the dots in padded satin stitch and the continuous line of scrolls that crosses the leafy motif in stem stitch.

The table napkins are worked in the same way, with a single motif only in one corner (top diagram).

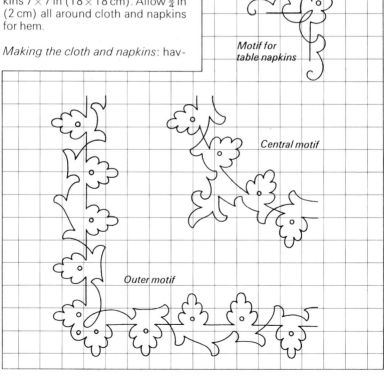

Motif for table napkins

Central motif

Outer motif

TOWEL SET

Materials: blue linen toweling (i.e. the same on both sides, such as huckaback); 1 skein of stranded cotton in each of the following colors: pink, dark red, white and shaded green; strong blue cotton.

Stitches: padded satin stitch (see page 76), stem stitch (see page 60), isolated overcast bars (see page 48), basting (see page 40), Paris stitch (see page 45), blind stitch (see page 54).

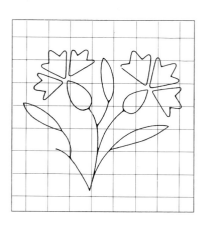

Measurements: small towel – about 25×16 in (64×40 cm); larger towel – about 43×25 in (108×25 cm). Allow an extra $3\frac{1}{4}$ in (8 cm) on all the short sides and $1\frac{1}{4}$ in (3 cm) on all the long sides.

Making the towels: having cut out the towels on the straight grain (see page 53), using the above measurements, turn in and baste $1\frac{1}{4}$ in (3 cm) on the sides of both towels and turn in and baste $3\frac{1}{4}$ in (8 cm) at one end as well. Hem (see pages 54–55) both sides of each towel. On the

basted end of each towel withdraw 3 fabric threads (see page 53) and work hem in isolated overcast bars. At the other end, turn up $3\frac{1}{4}$ in (8 cm) to the right side and baste very near to the fold. Now draw the flower motifs onto the turned-up border, using the diagram on the left for the smaller towel and the one on the right for the larger one. Remove basting and work the flowers and leaves in padded satin stitch and the stems in stem stitch.

Draw 2 in (5 cm) wide scallops on the right side of the fabric, using a saucer as a template, 6 in (15 cm) from the lower edge and fold the embroidered border up again, turning its raw edge under to follow exactly the curves of the scallops. Baste it down, and finish off by working a row of Paris stitches, in the strong blue thread, all the way along. Press the completed work under a damp cloth.

EMBROIDERY FOR CHILD'S CARDIGAN

Materials: 1-ply white wool and 1 skein of stranded embroidery cotton in each of the following colors: sky blue, yellow and green.

Stitches: padded satin stitch (see page 76), stem stitch (see page 60), and straight stitch (see page 73).

Measurements: the embroidery is about $2\frac{1}{2}$ in (22 cm) long and $1\frac{1}{4}$ in (3 cm) wide. The cardigan is for a 1-year-old child.

To work the embroidery: this can be done on most machine-knitted garments which are not already heavily patterned. Trace the design onto tissue paper and pin or baste in place onto sweater. Working through the tissue paper, with the white wool, work the buds and flower petals in padded satin stitch. taking care not to pull the yarn too tight. With the yellow embroidery thread, work the centers of the flowers in padded satin stitch, too. Now work the leaves with the green thread in stem stitch and put 2 straight stitches, in the same color, at the base of each bud. Finish off the tips of the petals and buds with 3 straight stitches in blue.

It is better not to press this type of embroidery at all as it might flatten and lose its elasticity.

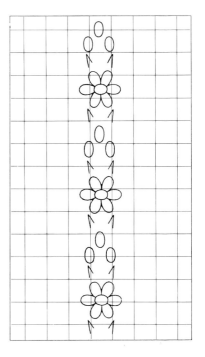

A BUNCH OF GRAPES
FOR A LADY'S CARDIGAN

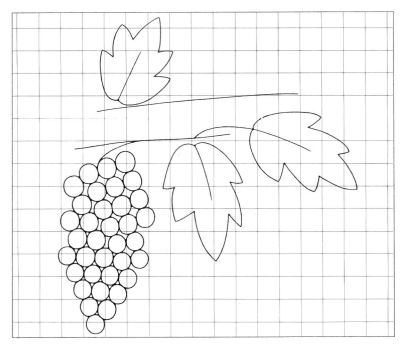

Materials: a few lengths of 4-ply wool in the following colors: red, mauve, green and beige.

Stitches: encroaching stem stitch (see page 60), padded satin stitch (see page 76), long and short satin stitch (see page 71).

Measurements: the embroidery measures $9 \times 6\frac{3}{4}$ in (23×17 cm) and the cardigan is a ladies' size.

To work the embroidery: the motif is shown on a handknitted cardigan. Trace the design onto tissue paper and pin or baste in place. Working through the tissue, work the branches and stems in encroaching stem stitch with the beige yarn and then embroider the grapes in padded satin stitch, mixing the red with the mauve, as in the illustration. Complete by working the leaves in satin stitch, embroidering over 2 or 3 knitted stitches at a time.

Although this type of embroidery is very simple to do, care must be taken to maintain an even tension which retains the elasticity of the knitted fabric. The same motif would look equally well on the front of a sweater, on the pockets of a cardigan, etc. Do not press.

SUN-BLIND

Materials: beige hessian; 3 skeins of stranded embroidery cotton in green, 4 in chestnut brown and 5 in shaded cotton from yellow to chestnut brown.

Stitches: padded satin stitch (see page 76) and stem stitch (see page 60).

Measurements: 110 × 50in (approx. 280 × 130 cm) plus 8 in (20 cm) for the top and bottom hems.

Making the sun-blind: as the narrower measurement given above is the usual width of hessian, the selvedges will be sufficient to finish off each side of the shade. If there are raw edges, however, turn ¾ in (2 cm) of fabric towards the wrong side and hem in the usual way.

First of all, ensure that the fabric is cut, on the straight grain (see page 53), to the measurements given above and turn up the hems at top and bottom, working them as explained on pages 54–55. Transfer the design which is shown vertically on this page onto the fabric starting 20 in (50 cm) from the top hem. The second motif should start 12 in (30 cm) from the lower edge of the first one and so on. Work the design in the two stitches suggested above, changing the colors as shown in the photograph. Now press the completed work on the wrong side, under a damp cloth.

To hang the blind at a door or window, make sure that there are two hooks or a rod support at each side of the top of the frame. Take a rod or bamboo pole 12 in (30 cm) longer than the width of the fabric and thread it through the top hem.

TABLECLOTH WITH LOZENGE MOTIFS

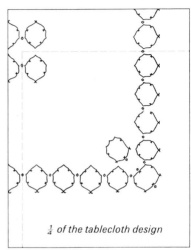

$\frac{1}{4}$ of the tablecloth design

Materials: even-weave embroidery cotton fabric and 4 skeins of stranded embroidery cotton in each of the following colors: green, yellow ochre and shaded yellow ochre.

Stitches: stem stitch (see page 60), padded satin stitch (see page 76), running stitch (see page 39). French knots (see page 80) and simple four-sided stitch (see page 47).

Measurements: 44 × 45 in (112 × 116 cm) plus $1\frac{1}{4}$ in (3 cm) all around for the hem.

Making the tablecloth: cut the cloth out, following the measurements given above and ensuring that it is on the straight grain (see page 53). Withdraw 2 fabric threads (see page 53), at a distance of $1\frac{1}{4}$ in (3 cm) from the edge, from all four sides.

Now count over 4 fabric threads and withdraw the next 2. Fold edge in three towards the right side, giving a hem of about $\frac{3}{8}$ in (1 cm). Complete with simple four-sided stitch.

Using the above diagrams as a guide, transfer the lozenge motifs onto the fabric arranged as shown; the dotted line on the right-hand diagram encloses one-quarter of the whole. Work the scrolled frames and one of the stems in stem stitch, the other two stems in running stitch, the small lozenges, leaves, flowers and the center of one flower in padded satin stitch and the center of the other two flowers in French knots.

Press the completed work on the wrong side on a well padded ironing board under a damp cloth to ensure that the design stands out well and is not flattened in any way.

CHRISTENING BAG

Materials: white cotton fabric; $3\frac{7}{8}$ yd (3.5 m) of white ribbon $\frac{3}{8}$ in (1 cm) wide; 22 in (55 cm) of white ribbon $1\frac{1}{8}$ in (3 cm) wide; 5 skeins of stranded embroidery cotton in white; strong white sewing thread; $5 \times \frac{3}{8}$ in (1 cm) covered buttons in white; $2\frac{1}{4}$ yd (2 cm) of ready-made broderie anglaise border lace.

Stitches: padded satin stitch (see page 76), French knots (see page 80), straight overcasting (see page 41), buttonhole stitch (see page 42) and backstitch (see page 40).

Measurements: the rectangle that covers the mattress measures $17\frac{3}{4} \times 24$ in (45×60 cm).

Making the christening bag: the basis of the bag is a small mattress, with a flat pillow attached, the whole thing being trimmed with ready-made broderie anglaise. The embroidered rectangle that covers the child is sewn on to the lower edge of the mattress by means of closely worked backstitching. The instructions given here are for the embroidery down the front which is worked on a separate strip and sewn on later.

First of all, cut out a rectangle from the cotton fabric, on the straight grain (see page 53), of 9×20 in (23×51 cm) and transfer the design from page 158 on to it. Embroider all the motifs with the white stranded cotton, remembering that the padding stitches (see page 39) for the satin stitch must be very close together. Now work the embroidery on the wider ribbon and edge it with scallops of buttonhole stitching. The buttonholing should be padded, in

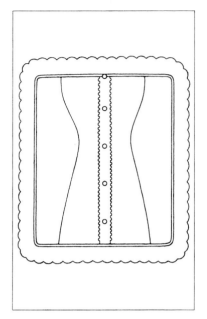

the same way as the satin stitch.

Cut out another rectangle of white cotton fabric, again ensuring that it is on the straight grain, for the cover. This should measure $17\frac{3}{4} \times 24$ in (45×60 cm) and sew it firmly, in small backstitching, to the lower edge of the mattress. Marking the center line first with a row of basting, sew the embroidered strip down the middle of the cover. Down the center of the embroidery, sew the embroidered ribbon and the buttons, as in the photograph.

The broderie anglaise edging can now be sewn into place all around the mattress in closely-worked backstitch. Wherever stitching is visible, such as on the broderie anglaise edging and the edges of the embroidered panel, it should be covered with the narrower ribbon.

158

TABLECLOTH AND
TABLE NAPKINS

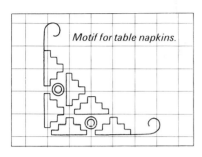

Motif for table napkins.

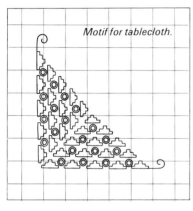

Motif for tablecloth.

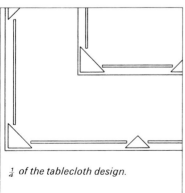

$\frac{1}{4}$ of the tablecloth design.

Materials: cotton embroidery fabric in yellow; 8 skeins of stranded embroidery cotton in white; strong white sewing thread.

Stitches: vertical satin stitch (see page 77), broderie anglaise (see page 72), simple hemstitch (see page 45), simple four-sided stitch (see page 47) and up-and-down stitch (see page 48).

Measurements: tablecloth measures 61 × 47 in (155 × 120 cm) and the napkins 13 × 13 in (33 × 33 cm) plus $\frac{3}{4}$ in (2 cm) for the hems.

Making the set: cut out the tablecloth and 6 napkins on the straight grain (see page 53). Withdraw 2 fabric threads (see page 53) at a distance of $\frac{3}{4}$ in (2 cm) from the edges of both the tablecloth and napkins. Fold the hems in half and work all around in simple hemstitching with the strong thread.

On the tablecloth, prepare two drawn-thread strips on which to work the four-sided stitch, the first $4\frac{3}{4}$ in (12 cm) and the second 15 in (38 cm) from the hemstitching; withdraw 2 fabric threads, leave 3 and withdraw another 2. Work the simple four-sided stitch over both strips of drawn thread.

Now transfer the motifs onto the positions shown in the diagrams and work them in broderie anglaise and vertical satin stitch.

Inside each rectangle bounded by the four-sided stitch-work, withdraw the requisite number of fabric threads for the up-and-down stitch, as shown in the bottom diagram.

The design is only used in one corner of each of the 6 table napkins, this being worked in vertical satin stitch and broderie anglaise.

CUSHION IN HOLBEIN AND ALGERIAN EYE STITCHES

Materials: yellow hessian; 1 skein of stranded embroidery cotton in red and brown; pillow form or cotton batting 16 × 12 in (40 × 30 cm); zipper or strip of Velcro; strong yellow sewing cotton.

Stitches: zig-zag Holbein stitch (see page 79), separate Algerian eye stitch (see page 81), straight stitch (see page 73) and backstitch (see page 40).

Measurements: 16 × 12 in (40 × 30 cm) plus 1¼ in (3 cm) for seams.

Making the cushion: cut out the two pieces of the cushion on the straight grain (see page 53). The embroidery is worked on one piece only of the cushion, starting with a large square in zig-zag Holbein stitch 2¼ in (7 cm) from the outside edge. Work a second square 2¼ in (7 cm) from the first, varying the design by making one stitch vertical and the next diagonal. The separate Algerian eye stitches can now be worked between the two frames, as shown in the diagram. Finally, embroider a design in straight stitches, as shown, in the center. Using the strong matching cotton and a small backstitch, join the two pieces together with right sides facing as follows: one short side, one long side, the other short side and then about 2 in (5 cm) at each end of the second long side. Turn work right side out and insert zipper and pillow form.

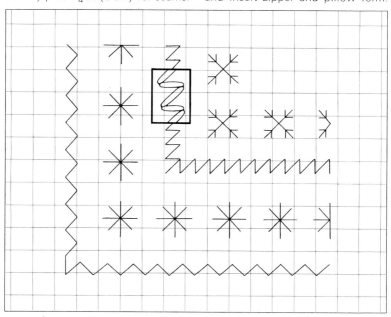

162

BABY'S BIB, BONNET AND SUMMER TOP DECORATION

Materials: 2 skeins of stranded embroidery cotton in white.

Stitches: padded satin stitch (see page 76) and shadow stitch (see page 79).

Measurements: the embroidery on the bib measures $4\frac{1}{4} \times 4\frac{1}{4}$ in 11 $\times$ 11 cm), $2\frac{1}{2} \times 1\frac{1}{4}$ in (6×3 cm) on the bonnet and $3\frac{1}{2} \times 1\frac{1}{2}$ in (9×4 cm) on the summer top.

Decorating the garments: the embroidery is worked on garments on which the scalloped edges have already been worked in buttonhole stitch. Transfer the designs onto the appropriate pieces by following the diagrams. On the bonnet, the embroidery is repeated on both sides and on the center front. The flowers, leaves and dots are worked in padded satin stitch and the decorative scrolls in shadow stitch.

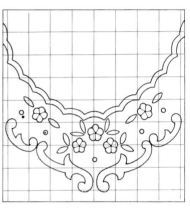

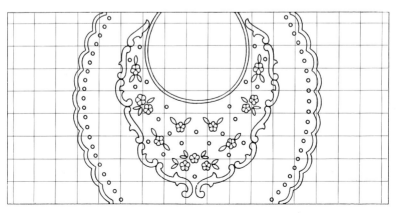

DRESSING-TABLE SET

Materials: white or natural organdy; 4 skeins of stranded embroidery cotton in sky blue.

Stitches: shadow stitch (see page 79), padded satin stitch (see page 76), buttonhole stitch (see page 42) and stem stitch (see page 60).

Measurements: the round mat (2 in set) is about 8 in (20 cm) in diameter and the oval mat measures about 18 × 12 in (45 × 30 cm). Allow an extra $\frac{3}{4}$ in (2 cm) all around which will be cut off when buttonhole stitching is complete.

Making the mats: draw the motifs lightly onto the back of the mats and work, still on the back, all the motifs in shadow stitch except the veins of the leaves, the flowers and the dots. The veins and large flowers are worked, on the right side, in stem stitch while the dots, small flowers and center of the large flower are in padded satin stitch, as can be seen in the illustration.

Now transfer the design of the outer edge of the mats onto the fabric, about $\frac{3}{4}$ in (2 cm) from the edge of the fabric. Work all around in ordinary buttonhole stitch and, when this is complete, cut away the excess fabric with small, sharp curved scissors, taking care not to cut into the stitches.

Press on the wrong side under a damp cloth with a hot iron. A little spray-starch will help to restore their crispness.

FLOWERS TO LIVEN UP AN APRON

Materials: 1 skein of stranded embroidery cotton in each of the following colors: white, yellow, red, green, pink and shaded orange.

Stitches: stem stitch (see page 60), padded satin stitch (see page 76) and French knots (see page 80).

Measurements: the spray of flowers covers an area of about 7×7 in $(18 \times 18$ cm$)$.

Working the flowers: the motif can be worked on both pockets of a ready-made apron. It could also be worked on oven gloves, potholders, tea-cloths and breakfast cloths, etc., to brighten up the kitchen and give that "matching" look which is so attractive.

Transfer the motif onto each pocket, making sure it comes exactly in the center. Using the colors as shown in the illustration, work the stems in stem stitch, the petals and leaves in padded satin stitch, the flower centers in French knots and padded satin stitch, as can be seen in the photograph.

Press on the wrong side on a well padded ironing board, using a damp cloth, but without using too much pressure to avoid flattening the embroidery.

CHILD'S BIB

Materials: an even-weave white cotton fabric; white toweling; 1 ball of pearl cotton (coton perlé) in yellow and a few lengths in dark blue, dark green, black and pink; about 40 in (1 m) of red bias binding; white and red sewing cotton.

Stitches: separate Algerian eye stitch (see page 81), stem stitch (see page 60), padded satin stitch (see page 76), running stitch (see page 39), whipstitching (see page 41) and backstitch (see page 40).

Measurements: see below.

Making the bib: cut out both materials, leaving $\frac{3}{4}$ in (2 cm) all around for the seams. Draw in the stars on the cotton fabric, arranging them as indicated on the diagram; embroider them in separate Algerian eye stitch using the yellow pearl cotton. Now draw in the cats and the moon and embroider them in stem stitch. The cats' noses, mouths and eyes are worked in satin stitch.

Join the two pieces of fabric together with right sides facing and work in small backstitch along the two sides, lower edge and shoulders, leaving the neck open.

Finish off the lower edge with bias binding folded in half, attaching it with a row of running stitches. Join the two fabrics at the neck, turn in the seam allowance and whipstitch neatly all around. Edge the neck with the remaining bias binding, leaving 10 in (25 cm) at each side for the ties. Complete the latter by whipstitching the edges of the free ends together.

2 in = 5 cm	$3\frac{1}{2}$ in = 9 cm
$2\frac{3}{8}$ in = 6 cm	$10\frac{1}{4}$ in = 26 cm
$2\frac{3}{4}$ in = 7 cm	$11\frac{3}{4}$ in = 30 cm
$3\frac{1}{8}$ in = 8 cm	$12\frac{1}{4}$ in = 31 cm

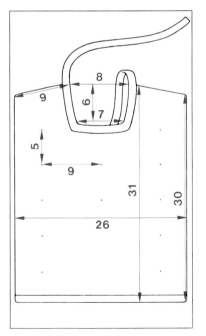

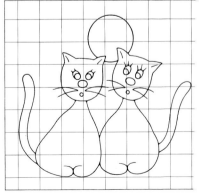

TABLECLOTH AND TABLE NAPKINS IN SINGLE FAGGOT STITCH

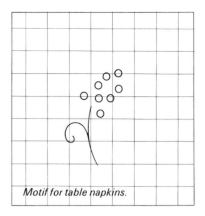

Motif for table napkins.

Materials: a finely woven cotton fabric in pink; 4 skeins of stranded embroidery cotton in green and 2 in red; strong pink sewing cotton.

Stitches: single faggot (two-sided square Holbein) stitch (see page 83), padded satin stitch (see page 76), stem stitch (see page 60) and simple hemstitch (see page 45).

Measurements: tablecloth about 33×33 in (84×84 cm), napkins $6\frac{1}{4} \times 6\frac{1}{4}$ in (16×16 cm) plus $\frac{3}{4}$ in (2 cm) on all sides for the hems.

Making the set: cut out the table-cloth and 6 napkins, on the straight grain (see page 53). Withdraw 2 fabric threads (see page 53) at a distance of $\frac{3}{4}$ in (2 cm) along all the sides, fold the hem back and work in

simple hemstitching all the way round the cloth and the napkins, using the pink sewing cotton.

Transfer the design to all four corners of the tablecloth and work one half of each leaf in single faggot stitch and the markings in the other half in satin stitch as well as the red berries. The stems and outlines of the leaves are worked in stem stitch.

On the napkins, the design is only transferred onto one corner of each of them and it is worked in the same way as on the tablecloth.

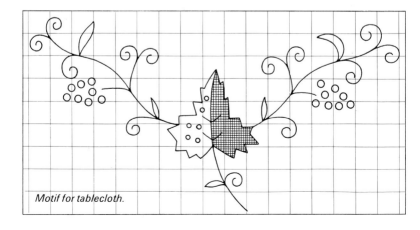

Motif for tablecloth.

SQUIRREL IN SWISS DARNING STITCH

Materials: a few lengths of 2-ply wool in beige and brown, and a tapestry needle.

Stitches: Swiss darning (see page 84).

Measurements: the squirrel covers an area of about $2\frac{3}{4}$ in (7 cm) and the sweater is for a 9-year-old child.

Working the squirrel: the squirrel illustrated has been worked on a machine-knitted garment but the same motif can, of course, be used to decorate or enliven a hand-knitted sweater, gloves or wooly hat. The design can also be enlarged by increasing the number of squares proportionately both in width and height.

To embroider the motif, use the beige wool and follow the diagram, working in Swiss darning stitch all the time. The eye is worked in the brown wool.

As this embroidery is worked in wool it is especially important to maintain an even, elastic tension throughout to ensure that the stitches cover the original stitches of the garment perfectly without pulling. The work should be pressed lightly on the wrong side under a damp cloth with a cool iron, to ensure that it does not become too flat and lose its character.

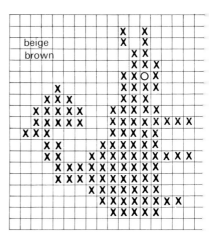

Bella Copia

TABLECLOTH AND TABLE NAPKINS IN SICILIAN DRAWN-THREAD STITCH

Materials: even-weave natural-colored linen and 30 skeins of stranded embroidery cotton in white.

Stitches: overcast bars in Sicilian drawn-thread work (see page 85) and basic buttonhole stitch (see page 42).

Measurements: the tablecloth measures 3×2 yd $(2.70 \times 1.80$ m) and the napkins $16\frac{1}{2} \times 16\frac{1}{2}$ in $(42 \times 42$ cm). Allow an extra 2 in (5 cm) all around, on both the cloth and napkins, which will be cut off after the edging has been worked.

Making the cloth and napkins: this handsome set, which could well become a family heirloom, is in fact remarkably simple to make. Although a beginner might find it a daunting task, nevertheless for someone with a little experience of drawn-thread work, it is well worth the time and concentration necessary to complete it. The cloth is an ideal size for a dinner party of up to twelve people and this means that the diagrams are relatively complex to follow, uniformity and symmetry being essential factors in their reproduction. However, once mastered, the main points to remember are to keep the stitches regular and the tension even throughout the work.

It is advisable to wash the fabric in hot water before cutting it. When nearly dry, it should be ironed with a fairly hot iron, on the wrong side.

This will avoid any shrinkage in laundering later, which would cause the embroidery to pucker disastrously. The cloth and napkins (12) can now be cut out, on the straight grain, according to the measurements given above, remembering to allow the extra 2 in (5 cm) all around.

The charts given on the following pages relate to one-quarter of the tablecloth and the weave is, of course represented in a reduced form by the squares. The chart opposite refers only to the motif for the napkins. To facilitate the work, it would be helpful to make a photocopy of pages 180–187 which all contain part of the design for the tablecloth. These can then be joined together by matching the letters A–D, as shown in the insert on page 180. In this way, you will have a complete quarter of the design to follow.

The design can now be transferred onto the fabric, using the photograph as a guide and being careful to match the various pieces up exactly. The design will, of course, have to be enlarged to the actual proportions of the cloth and great care taken to place the corner and central motifs symmetrically in position. The design can also be taken from the first chart (see page 177) and transferred to the corners of the napkins in the same way.

At this stage, cut and drawn-thread work can be started. Cut and withdraw the fabric threads (see page 53) as indicated in the diagrams by the areas "$\boxed{\cdot}$" and "$\boxed{\mathbf{x}}$" in the cloth and napkins. This will give you the basic network on which to work the overcast bars with the white embroidery cotton.

Having completed the main design, work a border on the outer edge of the embroidery in basic buttonhole stitch on the tablecloth and napkins, following closely the outlines shown on the charts. Finally, with a pair of pointed scissors, cut away all the excess fabric from the borders, taking great care not to cut into any of the buttonhole stitches.

The tablecloth and napkins can now be pressed with a hot iron on a well padded ironing-board, under a damp cloth. It is as well to use uniform pressure over the entire cloth, without exerting too much pressure in any one place, so as not to distort the embroidery. In order to obtain a well-ironed appearance, a little spray-starch can be applied at this stage; this will also ensure that the cloth "falls" better from the table thus showing the embroidery off to better advantage.

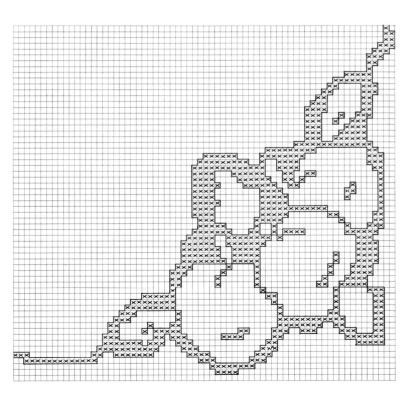

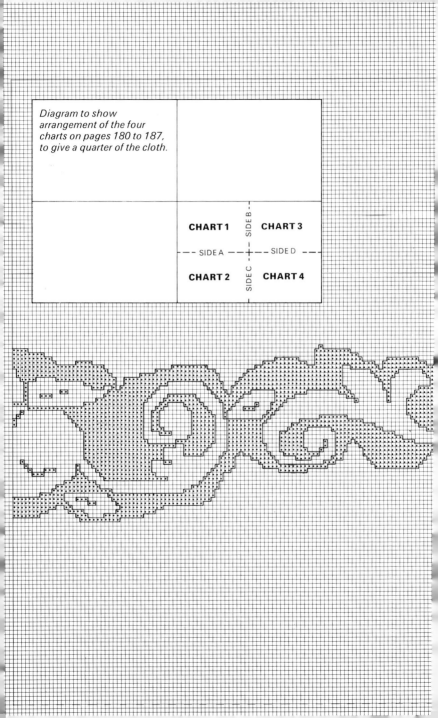

Diagram to show arrangement of the four charts on pages 180 to 187, to give a quarter of the cloth.

CHART 1 | SIDE B | CHART 3

--- SIDE A --- + --- SIDE D ---

SIDE C

CHART 2 | CHART 4

SIDE B

CHART 1

OUTER EDGE

SIDE B

CHART 3

SIDE D

SIDE D

CHART 4

SIDE C

WHITE BLOUSE EMBROIDERED IN OVERCAST WHEEL STITCH

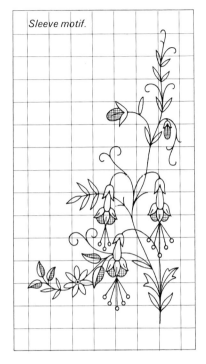

Sleeve motif.

Materials: 8 skeins of stranded embroidery cotton in white.

Stitches: overcast wheel stitch (see page 86), padded satin stitch (see page 76), faggot stitch (see page 83), stem stitch (see page 60), French knots (see page 80), straight overcasting (see page 41) and basic buttonhole stitch (see page 42).

Measurements: the blouse illustrated is a ladies' size, and the embroidery covers almost its entire front.

Working the decoration: the embroidery shown here has been worked on a very simple nineteenth-century shirt-blouse; the result is charming and modern but certainly not easy to achieve. It should only be attempted, therefore, by an experienced needlewoman.

The design on page 190 must first be drawn on the right front and then repeated in mirror image on the left front. The motifs can now be worked using the stitches listed above, as shown in the diagram and particularly in the photograph and detail on page 191.

The motif given on this page can now be drawn at the bottom of each sleeve, again using mirror images. The same stitches should be worked as on the two fronts, using the chart and photograph as guides.

The bottom edges of the shirt-blouse, sleeves and collar, are finished off with a row of overcast wheels and then with a scalloped border worked in buttonhole stitch at a distance of $\frac{3}{4}$ in (2 cm) from the outside edge. When these decorated borders have been completed, cut away the excess fabric with a small pair of sharp, curved scissors, being very careful not to cut into the embroidery.

It may seem superfluous to stress the need for perfect evenness in the stitches and in the tension, but its importance cannot be emphasized too much. The buttonhole stitching and satin stitch should be backed with closely worked padding stitch (see page 39) to make them stand out well.

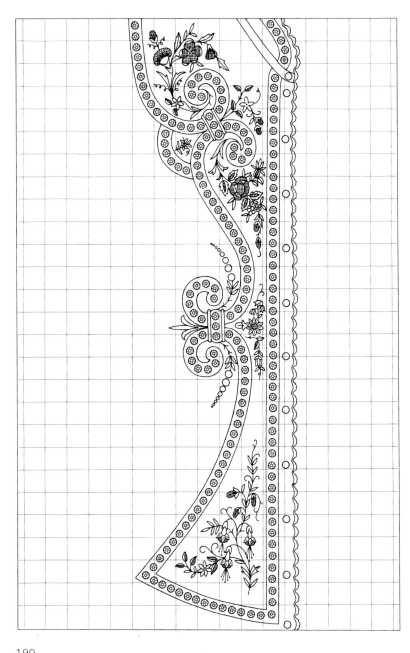

CURTAIN IN GUIPURE WORK

Materials: white cotton curtaining; 10 skeins of stranded embroidery cotton in white; strong white sewing cotton thread; curtain rings.

Stitches: guipure stitch (see page 86), up-and-down stitch (see page 48) and ladder hemstitch (see page 46).

Measurements: 70 × 60 in (170 × 150 cm) plus 1¼ in (3 cm) on all four sides for the hem.

Making the curtain: cut the fabric, on the straight grain (see page 53). Withdraw 4 fabric threads (see page 53) 1¼ in (3 cm) from the outer edge on all four sides; fold the hems back and work ladder hemstitching all the way round.

Working from the short sides, withdraw 15 fabric threads 12 in (30 cm) from the hemstitching and work in up-and-down stitch. At a distance of 14 in (35 cm) from the first up-and-down stitch withdraw another 15 fabric threads. Work a further row of up-and-down stitch on both sides and yet another row 6 in (15 cm) from the last two.

Transfer the designs as in the illustration and work them in guipure stitch. Cut the fabric away, to create the open-work, using small, curved scissors.

Using a hot iron, press carefully under a damp cloth. Sew the curtain rings to the top of the curtain and slide them over a curtain rod.

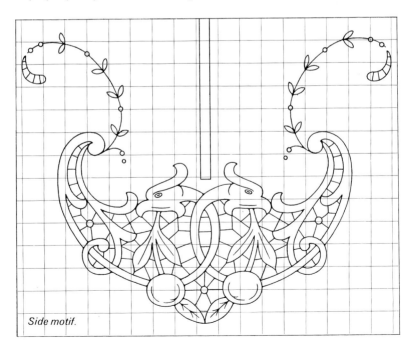

Side motif.

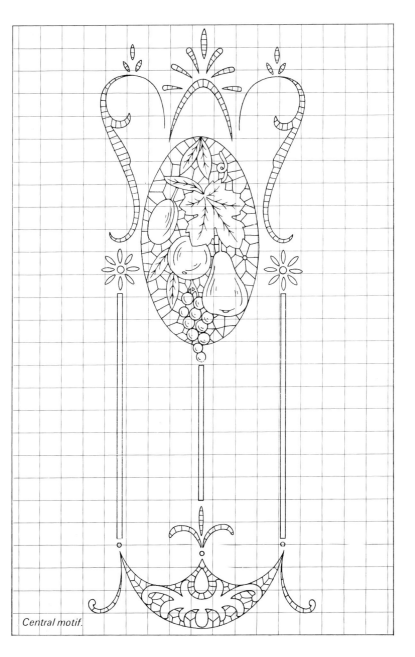

Central motif.

193

DAYTIME PILLOW COVER

Materials: white cotton embroidery fabric and 4 skeins of stranded embroidery cotton in white.

Stitches: guipure stitch (see page 86), stem stitch (see page 60) and basic buttonhole stitch (see page 42).

Measurements: 31 × 35 in (80 × 90 cm) plus ¾ in (2 cm) all around which will be cut away when the border has been worked.

Making the cover: cut out the rectangle, on the straight grain (see page 53). Transfer the design, of which one-quarter is given below, to the fabric ensuring that it is perfectly centered, with a ¾ in (2 cm) border all round. Work the main part of the design in guipure stitch. The veins of the leaves and details of the flowers are worked in stem stitch and the outer edge is worked in basic buttonhole stitch. Now cut away the excess fabric from the border and, with great care, all the small pieces from the design to give the effect of lace, as in the illustration.

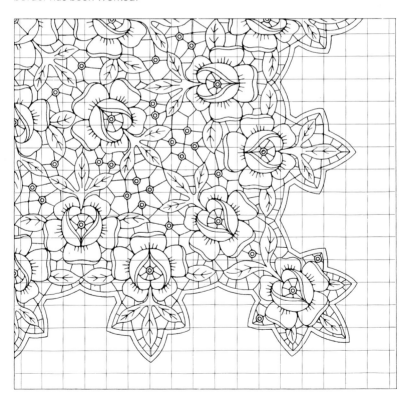

SMALL TABLECLOTH IN RENAISSANCE WORK

Materials: a piece of natural hessian or heavy linen; 22 yd (20 m) of Renaissance-work braid; 4 balls of pearl cotton (coton perlé) in white; strong beige cotton sewing thread of same thickness as fabric; waxed paper.

Stitches: Renaissance stitch (see page 88), encroaching stem stitch (see page 60), guipure stitch (see page 86), basic buttonhole stitch (see page 42) and whipstitching (see page 41).

Measurements: about 47 × 47 in (120 × 120 cm).

Making the cloth: first of all, draw the border design, taken from the diagram below, on to the waxed paper enlarging it to a depth of 10 in (25 cm). This is repeated along all four sides and at the corners. Baste

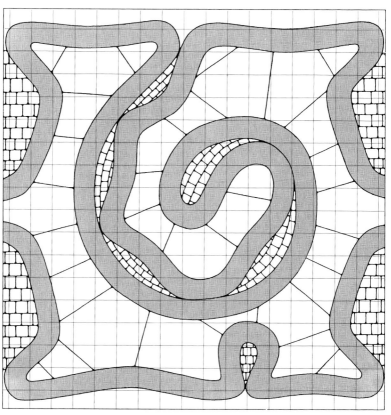

the braid onto the paper and work the linking bars. Now make the filling network, where necessary, as follows: the first row in basic buttonhole stitch, spacing the stitches about $\frac{3}{20}$ in (4 mm) apart and leaving the thread rather slack. On the return journey, which is obviously made in the opposite direction from the first row (right to left), work another row of buttonhole stitch, picking up the horizontal thread of each stitch in the previous row. Continue in this way until all the pieces of filling network have been completed.

When the border in Renaissance stitch has been worked, detach it from the waxed paper and place the fabric, which must be cut on the straight grain (see page 53), in the center. Whipstitch the two parts neatly together on the wrong side, using the strong thread.

Draw the grapevine design on each corner of the fabric and embroider it in guipure work and encroaching stem stitch. When all four corners are complete, cut away all the pieces very carefully to create the cut-work effect.

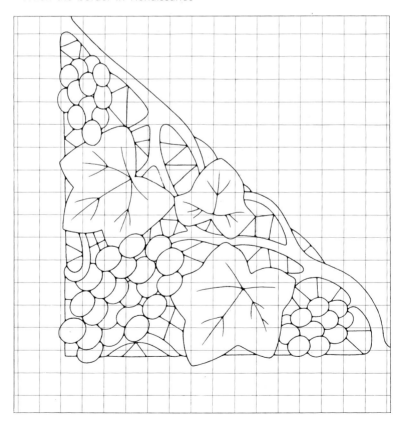

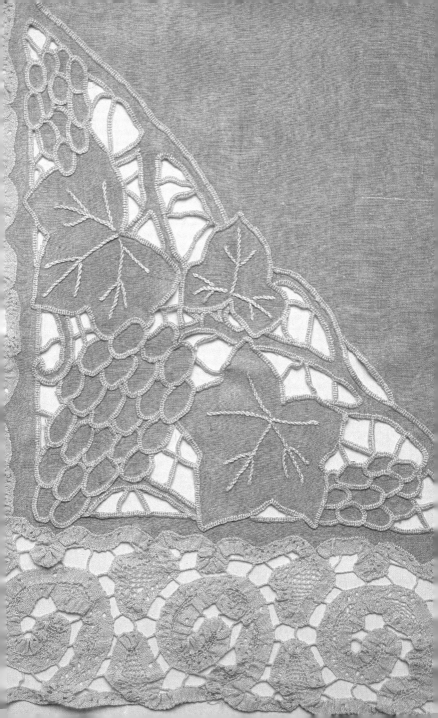

CHILD'S SMOCKED DRESS

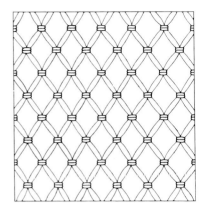

Materials: 2 skeins of stranded embroidery cotton thread in light blue, and 1 skein in pink, light green and aqua green.

Stitches: honeycomb smocking stitch (see page 91), stem stitch (see page 60), satin stitch (see page 76), basic buttonhole stitch (see page 42).

Measurements: the band of honeycomb smocking measures about $18\frac{1}{2} \times 3\frac{1}{4}$ in $(54 \times 8$ cm$)$ and the embroidery on the bodice covers an area of about 8×4 in $(20 \times 10$ cm$)$. The dress illustrated is for a 4-year-old child.

Working the smocking and embroidery: the bodice and skirt are worked in two separate pieces. First of all, prepare the skirt allowing considerably more fabric than usual to allow for the gathers (see pages 89–90) and work in honeycomb

stitch (about 20 rows), using the light blue thread. Now stitch the skirt to the bodice on which the flower and scroll motif is to be worked, making sure that it is placed centrally and $\frac{3}{4}$ in (2 cm) from the top row of smocking. The stalks and tendrils are in stem stitch while the flowers, leaves and scrolls are in satin stitch. The illustration can be used as a guide for changes of color. Finish off the sleeves and collar in buttonhole stitch and cut away the excess fabric.

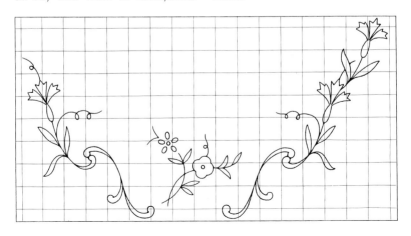

TULIPS IN CROSS STITCH

Materials: 1 skein of stranded embroidery cotton in green, red and royal blue.

Stitches: horizontal cross stitch (see page 93) and vertical cross stitch (see page 93).

Measurements: each flower covers an area of about $4 \times 2\frac{1}{2}$ in (10×6 cm). The dress illustrated is a ladies' size.

Working the embroidery: the embroidery in the photograph has been worked on the front pockets of a dress which needed livening up. The same motif would also look well on the patch-pockets of a skirt, on a breast pocket or on sleeves; it could also be used effectively to decorate oven gloves, cushions, a breakfast or trolley cloth, etc.

First of all, with a light touch, mark up the design in pencil on the fabric, using the appropriate sign for each color. Work the whole motif in vertical or horizontal cross stitch, depending on the arrangement of stitches, and changing the colors as indicated. Press the work (on the wrong side, if possible) on a well padded ironing-board under a damp cloth, being careful not to flatten the embroidery.

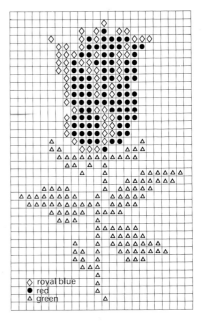

TABLECLOTH AND
TABLE NAPKINS

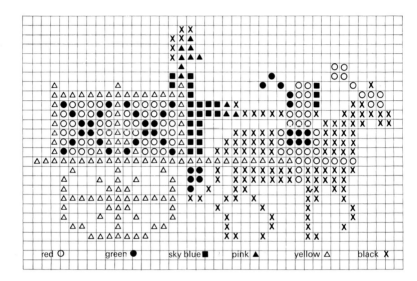

red ○   green ●   sky blue ■   pink ▲   yellow △   black X

Materials: natural linen embroidery fabric and 1 skein of stranded embroidery cotton thread in the following colors: red, green, brown, black, pink, yellow and sky blue.

Stitches: horizontal cross stitch (see page 93) and vertical cross stitch (see page 93).

Measurements: the tablecloth measures $27\frac{1}{2} \times 27\frac{1}{2}$ in (70×70 cm) and the table napkins 8×8 in (20×20 cm), including $\frac{3}{4}$ in (2 cm) all around for the fringe.

Making the set: cut out the cloth and 6 table napkins, on the straight grain (see page 53). Transfer the design for the smaller Sicilian cart from the chart on this page onto one corner of each table napkin $1\frac{1}{2}$ in (4 cm) from

the edge. Work in the colors indicated, using horizontal or vertical cross stitch according to the arrangement of the stitches. Now transfer all the motifs, given in chart form on pages 208 and 209, at a distance of $2\frac{3}{4}$ in (7 cm) from the edge. Work as described for the table napkins. Now work the square in the center of the cloth, with the little flowers at each corner (chart, lower right, page 209).

Finally, work a $\frac{3}{4}$ in (2 cm) fringe, following the explanation on page 112. Cut the left-over embroidery thread into pieces 2 in (5 cm) long and loop them through the edge between each group of the fabric threads, alternating the colors, and knot as the rest of the fringe.

Press the cloth and napkins on the wrong side, under a damp cloth.

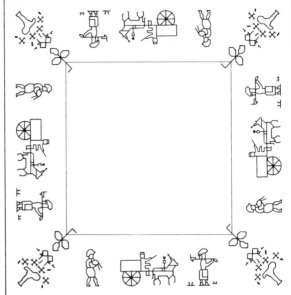

This little plan of the cloth shows the order in which the various designs on this and the opposite page should be worked.

△ yellow
■ light blue
O red
● green
✕ black
▲ pink
□ brown

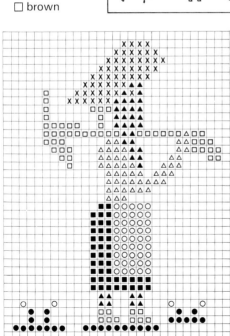

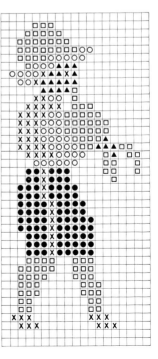

208

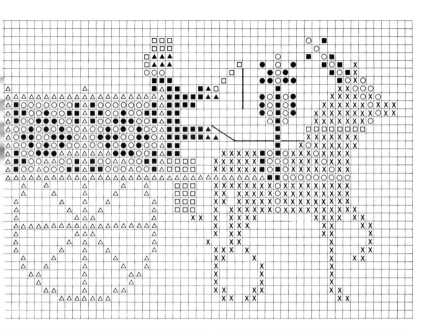

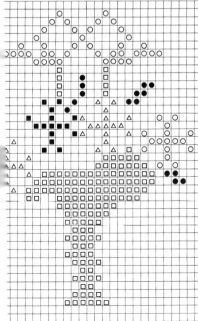

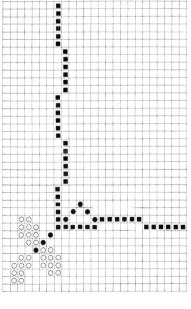

CUSHION IN CROSS STITCH

Measurements: 19 × 19 in (48 × 48 cm) plus ¾ in (2 cm) all around for the seams.

Materials: fairly heavy cotton embroidery fabric with an even weave; 2 balls of pearl cotton (coton perlé) in orange, green and sky blue; a 16 in (40 cm) zipper or strip of Velcro; a pillow form or cotton batting.

Stitches: horizontal cross stitch (see page 93), vertical cross stitch (see page 93) and backstitch (see page 40).

Making the cushion cover: cut out two identical pieces of fabric, on the straight grain (see page 53). On one piece only, transfer the whole design, of which a quarter is given below. Work in vertical or horizontal cross stitch, changing the colors as shown on the chart.

Join the two pieces of fabric with neat backstitching on three sides. Insert the zipper or strip of Velcro. Press under a damp cloth.

x orange
I orange
● sky blue
□ green

BABY'S SHEET AND PILLOWCASE

Materials: white cotton sheeting; 1 skein of pearl cotton (coton perlé) in each of the following colors: red, royal blue, green, orange and mauve; $3\frac{1}{4}$ yd (3 m) of royal blue ribbon; $3\frac{1}{4}$ yd (3 m) of broderie anglaise frilling with holes for ribbon; white sewing cotton thread of same thickness as fabric.

Stitches: horizontal cross stitch (see page 93), vertical cross stitch (see page 93), straight stitch (see page 73) and backstitch (see page 40).

Measurements: the sheet measures 63×47 in (160×120 cm) and the pillowcase 20×12 in (50×30 cm), plus another $\frac{1}{2}$ in (1 cm) all around both items for the hems.

Making the sheet: cut the fabric on the straight grain (see page 53), and turn in $\frac{1}{2}$ in (1 cm) on all four sides.

Using the sewing thread, work the hems as described on page 54.

Transfer the butterflies onto one end of the sheet. Work them all in vertical or horizontal cross stitch, according to the arrangement of the stitches. The antennae are made with straight stitches.

Backstitch the frilling onto the edge, using the sewing cotton, and thread the ribbon through the holes.

Making the pillowcase: cut out two identical pieces of fabric, on the straight grain, and join them on three sides, right sides facing, with neat backstitching. The case can now be turned right side out and some of the butterflies transferred onto it. They should be embroidered in the same way as on the sheet.

Neatly backstitch the frilling onto three sides of the pillowcase but, at the open end, it should only be attached to the top part so that the case remains open. Thread the ribbon through the holes.

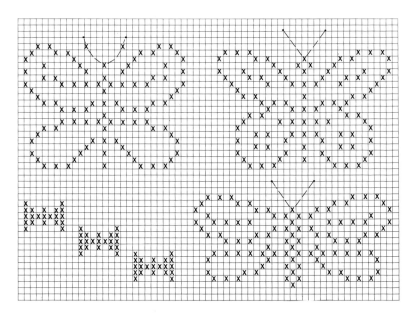

BEDSPREAD IN PERSIAN CROSS STITCH

Materials: woolen fabric with a fairly open but even weave (rather like a double-thread canvas) and 2 balls of pearl cotton thread (coton perlé) in green and brown.

Stitches: Persian cross stitch (see page 98) and simple hemstitch (see page 45).

Measurements: 95 × 63 in (240 × 160 cm) plus $\frac{3}{8}$ in (1 cm) for the hems.

Making the bedspread: having cut the fabric on the straight grain (see page 53), according to the measure-ments given above, turn up $\frac{3}{8}$ in (1 cm) all round. Do not withdraw any fabric threads but work in hemstitch.

When all the hems have been completed, work a row of Persian cross stitch in brown thread along each side of the coverlet, 8 in (20 cm) from the edge, working over 2 squares horizontally and 4 squares vertically. Now, starting from the top of the third vertical square, em-broider a row of Persian cross stitch in green thread just above the first row in such a way that they interlink.

Repeat the design twice more on the sides, leaving a space of 4 in (10 cm) between each double row, and once more at top and bottom. It is very important not to pull the thread too tight, when working this type of stitch, because it is easy for this sort of fabric to pull out of shape.

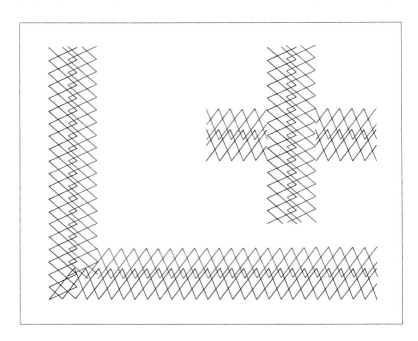

CASUAL HANDBAG
IN ARMENIAN
CROSS STITCH

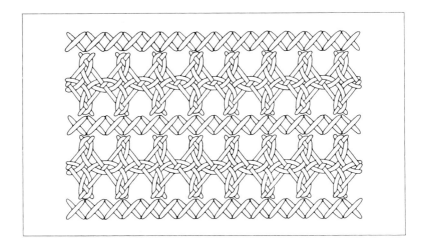

Materials: a piece of rather stiff muslin (No. 2); 2 balls of pearl cotton thread (coton perlé) in each of the following colors: sky blue, rust and yellow; blue cotton fabric for the lining; strong cotton sewing thread.

Stitches: Armenian cross stitch (see page 99), horizontal cross stitch (see page 93), backstitch (see page 40) and basting (see page 40).

Measurements: 20 × 8 in   (50 × 20 cm) plus ¾ in (2 cm) on all four sides for the seams.

Making the bag: ¾ in (2 cm) from the edge of one of the long sides and using the blue thread, work the first stage of Armenian cross stitch from left to right, the second from right to left using the rust thread and the yellow for the spirals. This stitch is worked over 2 horizontal and 4 vertical "squares". One unworked row should be left between each complete row of embroidery; these rows will be filled in later with horizontal cross stitch in alternate rows of sky blue and rust. With right sides together, fold the strip in half and join the short sides with backstitching. Join the bottom edges in the same way. Turn right side out and work a hem (see pages 54–55) around the top edge.

Cut the lining fabric to the same size as the main fabric, fold in half and join the short sides and the two bottom edges together. Turn right side out, press and insert into bag. Backstitch the lining onto the main fabric around the opening.

Cut 10 strands of 32 in (80 cm) of the pearl thread and braid them. Make a strap.

A USEFUL HOLD-ALL IN ASSISI WORK

Materials: white Assisi linen (or any linen with a fairly loose, even weave); 4 balls of pearl cotton thread (coton perlé) in both yellow and royal blue; strong white sewing thread in same thickness as fabric.

Stitches: Assisi work (see page 101), simple four-sided stitch (see page 47), basting (see page 40), and whipstitching (see page 41).

Measurements: the whole strip, which is folded into an envelope shape, measures about 11×22 in (28×55 cm) plus $\frac{3}{4}$ in (2 cm) all around for the hems.

Making the hold-all: having cut the linen, according to the above measurements, on the straight grain (see page 53), prepare the hems by withdrawing the fabric threads (see page 53) $\frac{3}{4}$ in (2 cm) from the edge, as follows: withdraw 2 threads, leave 3 and withdraw 2 more. Fold the outer border over twice, on the wrong side, and baste it with the strong sewing thread. Work all around the strip over the drawn work in simple four-sided stitch, using the yellow thread.

The Assisi work can now be started on the main area of the strip. It is, in fact, possible to work the design directly onto the fabric, without drawing it in first, just by following the chart and counting the threads. However, to be on the safe side, it is advisable to reproduce the design from pages 220–221 on squared paper and then to transfer it onto the fabric by tracing it with dressmaker's carbon paper (see page 34), making sure that it is perfectly centered. Complete all the motifs in Assisi work, using the yellow and blue threads as shown.

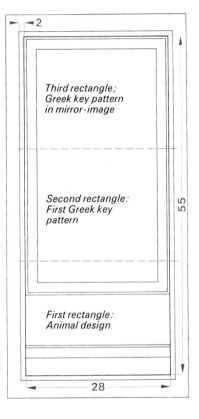

Third rectangle;
Greek key pattern
in mirror-image

Second rectangle:
First Greek key
pattern

First rectangle:
Animal design

2

55

28

Fold the strip in three, as indicated in the diagram on this page, to form an envelope, the flap of which is embroidered with the heraldic animal design. Join the sides of the two pieces which form the pocket, using the strong thread and neat backstitching.

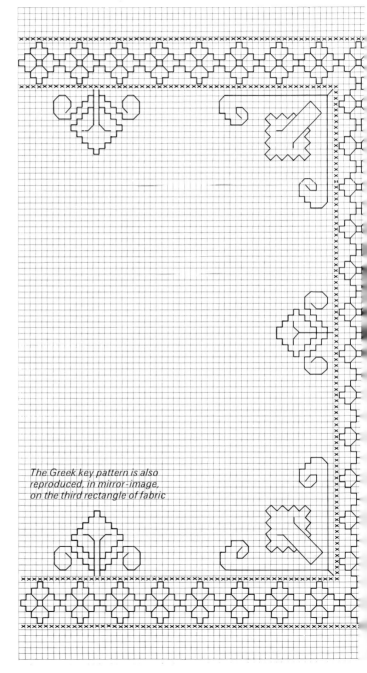

The Greek key pattern is also
reproduced, in mirror-image,
on the third rectangle of fabric

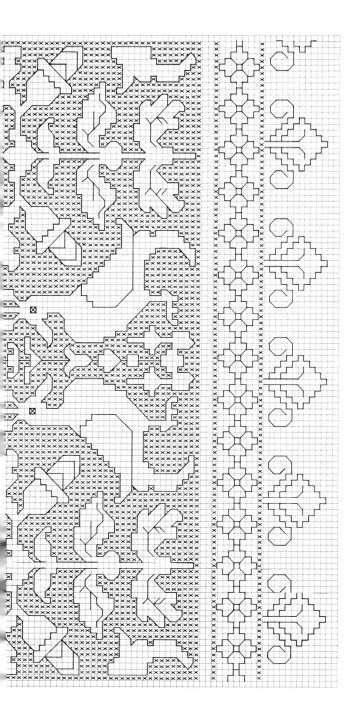

221

WALL-HANGING IN HALF GOBELIN STITCH

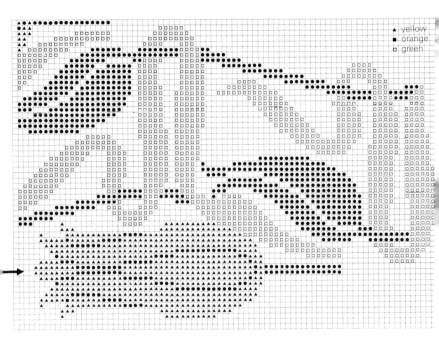

Materials: 10 squares to the inch double-thread canvas; 8 skeins of soft embroidery cotton in each of the following colors: green, orange, yellow and brick-red.

Stitches: half Gobelin stitch (see page 102).

Measurements: 14 × 9 in (38 × 22 cm) plus 1¼ in (3 cm) all around for mounting purposes.

Working the picture: following the chart, part of which is reproduced horizontally on this page, work the whole design, filling in the background with brick-red. It is advisable to start with the floral motifs and fill in the background last. The canvas must not be ironed. If there should be a little distortion when the work is complete, pull it gently into shape and leave it for a few hours under a clean sheet of paper with a weight on top.

The 1¼ in (3 cm) allowance is to enable the canvas to be stretched and fastened securely to a firm board so that it can be framed.

The arrow on the chart indicates the center of the design.

BOOK COVER IN STRAIGHT GOBELIN STITCH

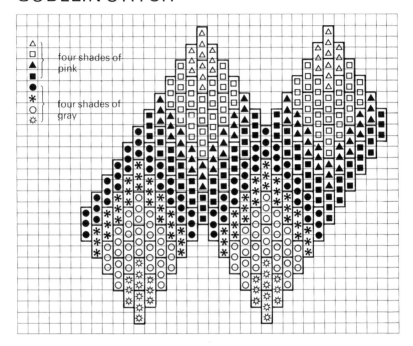

four shades of pink

four shades of gray

Materials: small meshed double-thread canvas; 2 skeins of soft embroidery cotton in each of the following colors: 4 shades of gray and 4 shades of pink; a piece of pearl gray silk for the lining.

Stitch: straight Gobelin stitch (see page 102).

Measurements: $11\frac{1}{2} \times 7\frac{1}{2}$ in (29 × 19 cm) plus $\frac{3}{4}$ in (2 cm) on all 4 sides which will remain unworked. These measurements, will of course, be adjusted according to the size of the book to be covered.

Working the cover: leaving $\frac{3}{4}$ in (2 cm) of border free all around, work the design in straight Gobelin stitch, following the chart carefully and changing color as indicated.

Glue the unworked edges of the canvas to the inside edges of the book cover and stretch the work well so that it is completely taut.

Now cut out 2 rectangles of gray silk about $7\frac{1}{2} \times 5\frac{3}{4}$ in (19 × 14.5 cm) and stick them over the inside of the front and back covers, being especially careful to cover the unworked canvas borders.

AN ELEGANT BOX
IN PETIT POINT

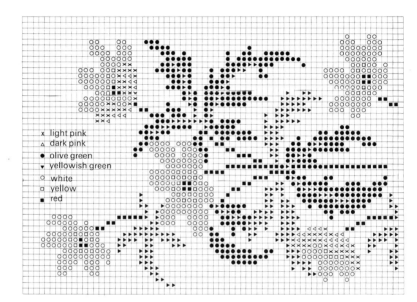

x light pink
△ dark pink
● olive green
▼ yellowish green
○ white
□ yellow
■ red

Materials: a piece of fine, single-thread canvas, $2\frac{1}{4}$ yd (2 m) of gold upholstery braid; a piece of green velvet; 3 balls of pearl cotton thread (coton perlé) in each of the following colors: white, yellow, beige, red, 2 shades of pink and 2 shades of green.

Stitch: petit point, first method (see page 103).

Measurements: the area of canvas worked here is about $4\frac{3}{4} \times 6\frac{3}{4}$ in (12×17 cm) plus $\frac{3}{8}$ in (1 cm) on all 4 sides which will remain unworked. These measurements can, of course, be adjusted for any desired size box.

Working the box: work the design in petit point (first method), taking care to change color as indicated in the chart on this page and repeating the design as necessary. It is advisable to work the flowers and leaves first and then fill in the background in beige.

When the canvas work is complete, spread glue all over the top of the box-lid. Stretch the embroidered canvas carefully over the top, turn the unworked borders to the inside and glue them down.

Next, cut out a piece of velvet to go round the box and glue into place. Finally, stick the gold braid around the edges of the box.

WASTEPAPER BASKET IN TENT STITCH

Materials: double-thread canvas; 1 skein of soft embroidery cotton in each of the following colors: gold, white, 2 shades of red, 2 shades of pink, 2 shades of sky blue, 2 shades of salmon pink, 2 shades of violet and 2 shades of yellow, 2 skeins in green and 15 in beige; a piece of red velvet; 60 in (1.5 m) red upholstery braid; fabric glue.

Stitch: tent stitch, method No. 2 (see page 103).

Measurements: the strip used here measures $28\frac{3}{4} \times 4\frac{3}{4}$ in $(73 \times 12$ cm) plus $\frac{3}{4}$ in (2 cm) on the 2 long sides which will remain unworked. These measurements can be adjusted to cover any desired size box.

Instructions: it is advisable to work the flowers first, starting from the center of each flower and working outwards, to give a more even appearance. When all the flowers, have been worked, the background can be filled in using the beige thread.

Mark out a central band $6\frac{1}{4}$ in (16 cm) deep and spread the glue over it. Leave to set slightly for a few minutes and then carefully stretch the embroidered canvas onto it, holding it by the unworked edges. When the strip is correctly placed, spread the glue all over the rest of the outside of the container and apply the velvet, covering the 2 bands of unworked canvas. Complete by applying 4 strips of braid, as shown in the photograph.

□ light shades: yellow, pink, red, sky blue, salmon pink, violet
● dark shades: yellow, pink, red, sky blue, salmon pink, violet
△ green   ○ gold   ◆ white

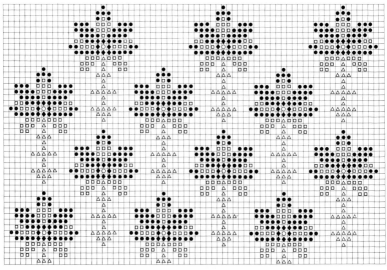

DRUM LAMPSHADE IN WOVEN STITCH

Materials: double-thread canvas;
3.5 oz (100 g) of 4-ply wool in gray
and 3.5 oz (100 g) in dark red; a pair
of lampshade rings 37 in (94 cm) in
circumference; a piece of fairly stiff
lampshade paper 80 in (2 m) of
beige bias binding; fabric glue.

Stitch: woven stitch (see page 104).

Measurements: the strip for the
lampshade measures 37 × 12 in
(94 × 31 cm) plus 2¾ in (7 cm) on
the 2 long sides which will remain
unworked.

Making the lampshade: leaving an
unworked strip of 2¾ in (7 cm), work
the border in the lozenge pattern,
following the diagram below and
changing color as indicated. Now
work the other pattern, leaving 7
lines of canvas unworked between
every 7 rows of open woven stitch.
Having worked 7 strips leave a further 7 lines unworked and repeat the
closely worked strip for the lower
border.

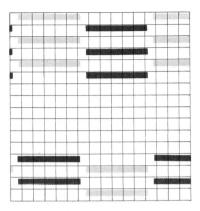

Cut the lampshade paper to the
same size as the embroidered canvas, spread the fabric glue over it and
stick the canvas in position, making
sure that it is stretched perfectly
straight. The unworked canvas will
project at top and bottom. Fold this
to the inside, glue and press down
firmly.

Bind the two rings with the bias
binding and join the ends with a few
stitches. Spread some fabric glue
over the binding and attach the
lampshade paper, pressing it firmly
with the fingers; ⅜ in (1 cm) of the
paper should project above and
below the rings to hide the binding
rings.

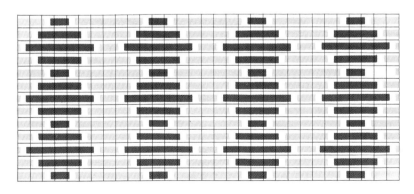

PICTURE-FRAME IN FLORENTINE (FLAME) STITCH

Materials: small gauge single-thread canvas; 5 skeins of stranded embroidery cotton thread in 5 shades of pink and 2 skeins in olive green; 48 in (120 cm) of upholstery cord to match; a piece of beige silk.

Stitches: Florentine stitch (see page 105) and tent stitch, method No. 1 (see page 103).

Measurements: the frame measures 7 × 6¼ in (18 × 16 cm) plus ¾ in (2 cm) on all four sides which will remain unworked.

Making the frame: the chart represents one-quarter of the frame and it must be remembered that, as each Florentine stitch is worked over 4 vertical threads, 4 symbols correspond to one stitch. Work the sides of the frame in Florentine stitch and fill in the corners in tent stitch (method No. 1) using the olive green thread.

Leaving ¾ in (2 cm) of unworked canvas on the inside of the frame, cut away the rest of the central canvas.

To make the frame you will need: two pieces of stiff cardboard 7 × 6¼ in (18 × 16 cm), one with a 1⅛ in (3 cm) and the other with a ¾ in (2 cm) border, a piece of cardboard 5½ × 4¾ in (14 × 12 cm) and a piece of glass 5¾ × 4⅞ in (14.5 × 12.5 cm). Glue the embroidered canvas onto the wider frame, folding the canvas border to the back. Cover separately the two remaining pieces of cardboard with the beige silk. Glue the silk-covered frame to the back of the embroidery-covered frame and insert the glass. Finish off the outer and inner edges of the embroidery with the upholstery cord and put the other piece of silk-covered card behind the glass.

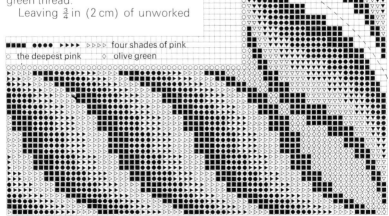

■■■■ ●●●● ▶▶▶▶ ▷▷▷▷ four shades of pink
○ the deepest pink   ◇ olive green

FLOOR RUG IN SMYRNA STITCH

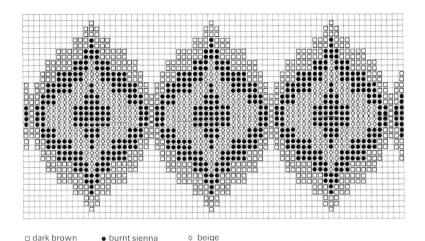

□ dark brown   ● burnt sienna   ◊ beige

Materials: double-thread rug canvas; $2\frac{1}{4}$ lb (1 kg) rug wool in each of the following colors: beige, burnt sienna and dark brown.

Stitches: Smyrna stitch (see page 107), straight overcasting (see page 41).

Measurements: the pile area here measures $61\frac{1}{2} \times 35\frac{1}{2}$ in (156 × 90 cm) plus $1\frac{1}{4}$ in (3 cm) all around for the border. These measurements can be changed to any desired size.

Making the rug: leaving $2\frac{1}{2}$ in (6 cm) of unworked canvas on all four sides, work the whole rug in Smyrna stitch. It will be necessary to use a wooden gauge $\frac{3}{4}$ in (2 cm) wide to obtain a pile of the correct depth. The chart gives all the necessary color changes and the partial lozenge shapes at the edges can

either be worked in burnt sienna, as in the photograph, or in all three shades by following the relevant parts of the chart.

Fold the unworked canvas border in half and cover it completely with straight overcasting, using the darkest color. This should be worked into the row of holes next to the Smyrna stitches and extended out over the folded edge.

This rug is not difficult to make and the only problem may be its weight as you are working and the care that must be exercised as the loops are cut. To obtain a nice even pile, the stitches must be cut accurately in the middle in order to give a depth of $\frac{3}{4}$ in (2 cm).

TOWELS WITH APPLIQUÉ FLOWERS

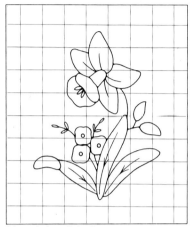

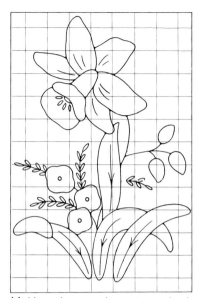

Materials: pink linen toweling and some white cotton fabric; stranded embroidery cotton in white; strong sewing cotton, of same thickness as the toweling, in pink.

Stitches: basic buttonhole stitch (see page 42), stem stitch (see page 60), padded satin stitch (see page 76), lazy daisy stitch (see page 65), hem-stitching with isolated overcast bars (see page 48) and basting (see page 40).

Measurements: the large towel measures 36 × 20 in (90 × 50 cm) and the appliqué work on it covers an area of 8 × 6½ in (20 × 16 cm). The small towel measures 22 × 13½ in (55 × 34 cm) and the appliqué work on it covers an area of 5 × 4 in (13 × 10 cm). Allow an extra 2 in (5 cm) at the top and bottom of both towels for hems and ¼ in (½ cm) on each side, unless there are selvedges.

Making the towels: cut out both towels from the pink linen, ensuring that they are on the straight grain (see page 53). Make the side hems where there is no selvedge by turning ¼ in (½ cm) to the back and working as described on pages 54–55. Now fold back 2 in (5 cm) at each end and hemstitch, with overcast bars, at the top and bottom.

Draw the floral motifs onto the white fabric and then, without cutting them out, baste them onto the towels. Center the motifs accurately and work the basting quite close to the outlines of the designs. Complete the appliqué by working in very close buttonhole stitch over the basting.

The excess cotton fabric can now be cut away with very sharp, curved scissors.

Finally, work the center of the flowers in satin stitch, the stems and leaf veins in stem stitch, and the small leaves in lazy daisy stitch.

APPLIQUÉ
CHERRIES

Materials: two small pieces of red felt; some lengths of pearl embroidery cotton (coton perlé) in 3 shades of green; some stranded embroidery cotton in red.

Stitches: stem stitch (see page 60), basting (see page 40) and backstitch (see page 40).

Measurements: the embroidery covers an area of 10 × 8 in (25 × 20 cm) and the diameter of the cherries is shown in the diagram.

To make the cherries; although this appliqué work is shown on the back of a child's bathrobe it could, of course, also be adapted to a similar garment for an adult. The position is a matter of choice as it could also look effective on the front, on the pockets or even on the hood.

Using the diagram as a guide to measurements, cut out the two cherries and baste them into position on the robe. There is no need to turn the edges in as this type of fabric does not fray. Using stem stitch and red embroidery thread, work all round the cherries.

To make the stalks, cut four 24 in (60 cm) lengths of all three shades of green pearl embroidery thread and braid them. Pin each of these to the top of the cherries and place in position as shown in the diagram, to include the leaves. Attach to the robe with neat backstitching along the center of the stalks and leaf outlines. Finally work the vein of the leaves in stem stitch.

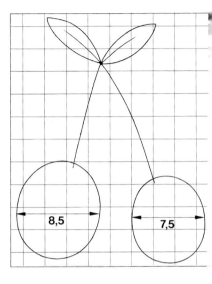

3 in = 7.5 cm
3$\frac{3}{8}$ in = 8.5 cm

TOY BAG

Materials: a piece of burlap, a piece of red and white gingham, a small piece of red cotton fabric (piqué type); 1 skein of stranded embroidery cotton thread in black; strong sewing thread in white, red and tan; about 3 yd (3 m) of red cord.

Stitches: basic buttonhole stitch (see page 42), basic stem stitch (see page 60), vertical satin stitch (see page 77), backstitch (see page 40) and basting (see page 40).

Measurements: the bag measures about 24×22 in (60×55 cm) plus $\frac{3}{4}$ in (2 cm) all around for the seams; the elephant covers an area of about 17×5 in (44×32 cm), its ear measuring about 8×5 in (20×13 cm), and a $\frac{3}{8}$ in (1 cm) border must be allowed all around the elephant and its ear.

Making the bag: cut the two sides of the bag from the burlap, according to the measurements given above (it can be made from one long strip, in which case side and top seams only need be allowed for). Cut similar

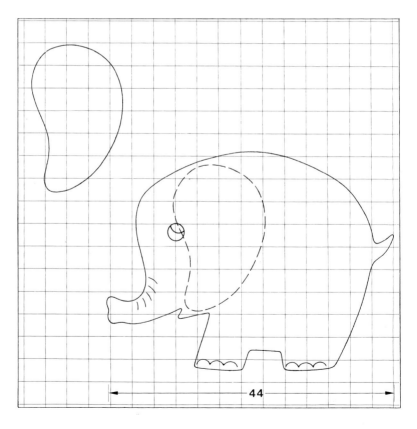

44

pieces (or one piece only, as just explained) from the gingham to make the lining. Both hessian and gingham must be cut on the straight grain (see page 53).

Now draw the shape of the elephant on a piece of tissue paper and draw its ear separately, using the diagram as a guide. Transfer the elephant drawing on to a piece of the gingham and cut out, leaving a border of $\frac{3}{8}$ in (1 cm) all around the motif. Baste the elephant onto one of the pieces of burlap (if this is in strip form, the elephant's feet will be nearest the center fold). Transfer the ear onto both the red fabric and the gingham; cut them both out, leaving a margin of $\frac{3}{8}$ in (1 cm) all around and join them together, right sides facing, with neat backstitching or by machine, leaving a few inches (centimeters) open at the top. Turn the ear right side out and finish it off all around the edge with either a row of backstitching or machine stitching in the strong red sewing thread.

The elephant can now be sewn into position with fairly wide-spaced buttonhole stitching. Attach the ear, as shown in the diagram, the plain red fabric outwards, by backstitching it to the elephant along the section that was left open.

Draw in the eye and feet, as shown in the diagram, and work them respectively in vertical satin stitch and stem stitch.

Seam the sides of the burlap bag, right sides together, using either a close backstitch or machine stitching and leaving about 5 in (13 cm) open on each side at the top. Repeat the process with the gingham. Turn the burlap sack right side out, slip the gingham one into it and join them together along the top and side openings, leaving about $\frac{1}{2}$ in (1.25 cm) open at the base of the latter. Make a casing for the cord by working 2 rows of stitches on both back and front between the openings. Cut the cord in half and thread one piece through the front and the other through the back. Knot the ends together at each side. Press all the work, including the appliqué design, with a hot iron, under a damp cloth.

Monograms
and alphabets

MONOGRAMS

It can be great fun and very worthwhile to see how original you can be in designing attractive ways of making an ornamental motif from your initials or those of a friend. The result is distinctive and gives even the simplest items such as sweaters, tee-shirts, bathrobes, blouses, bed linen, handkerchiefs, etc., an air of individuality.

It is not always easy to combine two or three letters in such a way as to create a well-balanced symbol which is not commonplace and yet, at the same time, is graphically acceptable. Sometimes the shapes of certain letters that form initials seem to be incompatible but this is a challenge to be faced and, sooner or later, a solution will emerge.

It would be impossible to give examples of every combination of letters and styles as they are limitless. However, it is hoped that the selection given here will provide inspiration for your own inventiveness. Some are very simple, geometric and modern; others are more elaborate, graceful and romantic, inspired by traditional tastes; and there are some which are quite eccentric, based rather on the style of advertising graphics.

A word of warning, do not be daunted by all the little flowers, curlicues and embellishments that so delighted our great-grandparents and which are returning so strongly into favor. The letters themselves are worked in either satin stitch or straight overcasting, the flowers are in satin stitch, the leaves in lazy daisy, while the stems and all the narrow lines are in stem stitch.

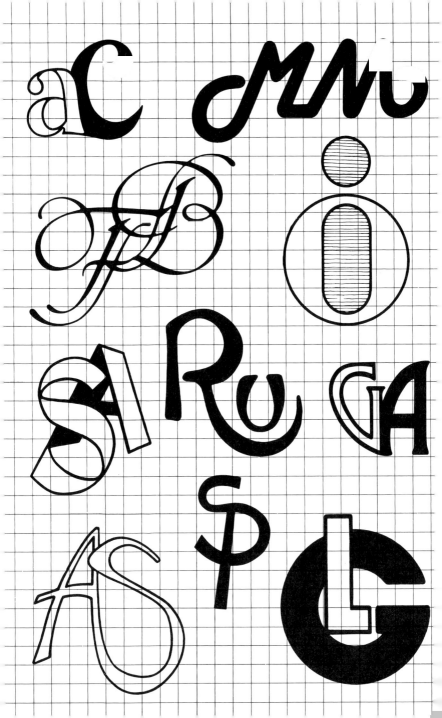

ALPHABETS

Here are some styles of letters and figures which lend themselves to being embroidered. They offer a wide choice of combinations to be made up into names or phrases.

The first alphabet on this page can be worked in cross stitch or some of the Gobelin stitches; the others are suitable for satin stitch, if very distinct outlines are wanted, while stem stitch or chain stitch would produce softer outlines. Several types of stitch are often combined when working letters. For example, outlines may be worked in satin stitch or straight overcasting while faggot stitch and the herringbone stitches are suitable for filling. Particularly pleasing shaded effects can be achieved by working the finer lines in stem stitch and the broader ones in satin stitch.

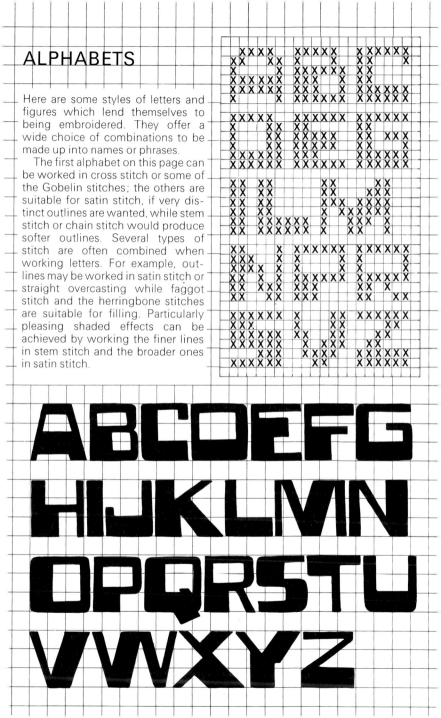

ABCDEFG
HIJKLMN
OPQRSTU
VWXYZ 12
34567890

abcdefghij
klmnopqr
stuvwxyz

INDEX

tent stitch *see under* Gobelin stitch
thimble 23
thread 16–20, 58
towels; set 146, *147*; with appliqué
   flowers 236, *237*
toy bag 240, *241*, 242
tracing; carbon paper 33, 34, 219;
   charcoal, powdered 33, 35; on
   corners 37–8; on glass 33, 36;
   thumbnail 33, 37; transfer 33, 34,
   37, 92
tracing wheel 33, 35
traycloths, round 120, *121*
Turkish stitch 47

twisted bars *see* overcast bars

up-and-down stitch 48, 160, 192

wall-hanging in half Gobelin stitch
   222, *223*
washing; embroidery 31–2; fabrics
   28, 30
wastepaper basket in tent stitch
   228, *229*
waxed paper 22, 24, 87, 88, 89
whipstitching 39, 41, 55, 88, 170,
   198, 218
woven stitch 77, 104, 230